A Blackbird's Year

Mind in Nature

Miles Richardson

Published in 2014 by FeedARead.com Publishing.

Text and map © Miles Richardson
Foreword © Rebecca Welshman
Illustrations & cover design © Danielle Callaghan
www.daniellecallaghan.com

The author or authors assert their moral right under the Copyright, Designs and Patents Act, 1988, to be identified as the author or authors of this work.

All rights reserved. No part of this publication may be reproduced, copied, stored in a retrieval system, or transmitted, in any form or by any means, without the prior written consent of the copyright holder, nor be otherwise circulated in any form of binding or cover other than that in which it is published and without a similar condition being imposed on the subsequent purchaser.

British Library C.I.P.

A CIP catalogue record for this title is available from the British Library.

Contents

Map of My Local Places of Mind
Foreword

1 Searching for New Year
2 Mind and Nature
3 Calling Rooks
4 Biopsychophysis
5 Flesh
6 Lived Mountains
7 Fragments of Summer
8 Being
9 Flatlands
10 Patterns of Nature

Acknowledgments

My Local Places of Mind

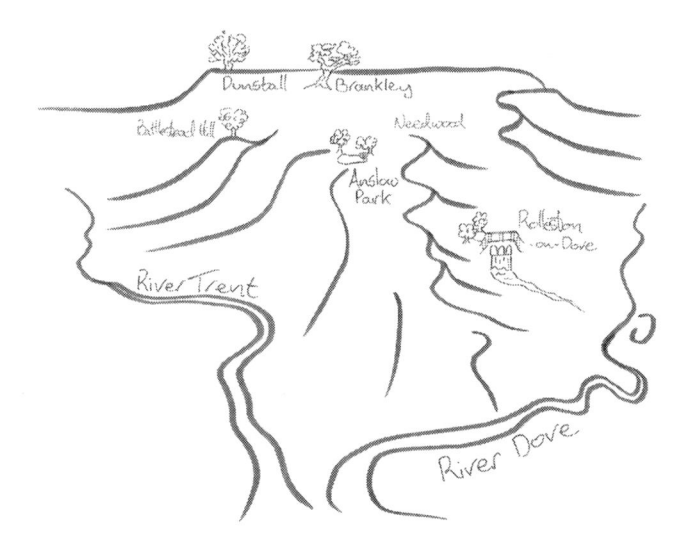

Foreword

By Rebecca Welshman

    This genuine and deeply considered exploration into the meeting places between nature and mind is a compelling and sensitive read. *A Blackbird's Year* charts a journey into a local rural area and explores the connections between nature and thought. The book explores how mind and nature inhabit one another – how experiencing nature illuminates the subtle nature of being and the processes of mind.

    Miles Richardson is an ergonomist and chartered psychologist and his recent research considers mindful and reflective attention to nature. *A Blackbird's Year* follows his earlier book *Needwood: A Search for Deep Nature*, which identifies the universal need for nature connection. In ten chapters Miles introduces us to new paradigms of thought to conceptualise the complex rhythms and pulses of connection experienced in the midst of nature.

    Guided by the philosophy of the Victorian naturalist and philosopher Richard Jefferies, this atmospheric and unique account takes time to consider the reality of individual trees, birds, and other natural phenomena. Having studied the works of the Richard Jefferies for more than a decade, with his works being the subject of my Doctoral thesis on literature, landscape and mind, it is exciting to see new books which seek to continue and develop the experiential aspects of his work. Other contemporary authors influenced by Jefferies include Richard Mabey and Robert MacFarlane. In his deep exploration into the heart of nature, Miles recognises the need to transcend the traditional parameters of contemporary autobiography, and in doing so successfully avoids nostalgia. Furthermore, in recognising footpaths in the landscape as channels within the mind, Miles unfolds new territory of individual conscious experience. Elements of this book thus remind me of Jefferies' spiritual autobiography *The Story of My Heart* (1883). Indeed, Jefferies has been very much a source of guidance, with quotations from his works at the beginning of each chapter.

Miles' experience as a researcher into the psychology of nature provides a sound basis for some of the ideas he introduces, such as 'biopsychophysis, a unity of life, mind, and nature'. Miles aligns and merges the meeting places between research and creativity with skill and precision, so that the two complement one another. In doing so he achieves something new – a style and concept in the tradition of Jefferies, but very much based in contemporary pertinent questions of the relations between mind and the surrounding world of matter, and the biology of consciousness. Miles identifies connections between the sights and sounds of nature and the flesh of the body, so that the skin becomes the place 'where body makes sense of wider nature'.

Miles' deep love and appreciation of nature is apparent in the various landscapes which he explores. His search takes the reader into the area of Needwood, near the River Dove. The small woodland at Brook Hollows is somewhere Miles has known since childhood – 'a wood that became smaller as I grew, but has regrown as I've learnt how to see with the fascination of a child.' The book also visits Fife, Northumberland, Devon, Coniston, and Holme in Norfolk.

Miles is keenly aware of the movements, sounds, and changing atmospheres of the natural world. He aligns himself to the 'power of the landscape', the dynamic energies of its daily presence, and the flowing importance of the senses, without which there would be no landscape. Through these subtle processes of sensual appreciation and recognition of the cosmic reality of the material, the writing gives shape to that rich and often fleeting sense of everything being harmonically balanced. The flight of a kingfisher, for example, or a raindrop on a branch, can somehow embody the whole of nature in a single perfect form.

One of the unique points of this book is the range of references which widen the response to nature. These include allusions to digital and analogue technologies, audio pyrotechnics, galaxies and space-time, a tree as a 'neural network', and the hearing of sound in colour – so that the Blackbird's notes are 'spotted white'. Miles' unfolding awareness reminds us that a landscape is never static but fluid, so that one thing can easily become another, such as 'the last leaves of a young oak [which] flew to become blue tits'.

Overall, the book suggests that we need to think more about mind in order to more fully understand our place in nature. This can be achieved through the wonderfully simple process of wandering through a local landscape, describing the joy of nature experience. The Blackbird is ever present in sight, sound, or mood, and thus becomes a symbol of consciousness.

A Blackbird's Year is significant as a new experiment in creative thought and for furthering our understanding of contemporary nature connection. As a creative writer and researcher I understand how difficult these books can be to write – how important it is to successfully negotiate the balance between nature description and individual perception. Miles achieves this, and in doing so demonstrates how writing creatively about the natural world is not simply a process of consciousness but a craft that can actively shape consciousness itself.

> Dr Rebecca Welshman, Honorary Fellow, Centre for Research into Reading and Linguistic Systems, Department of Psychology, University of Liverpool.
> Co-author (with Hugoe Matthews), *Richard Jefferies: an Anthology* (2010).

Chapter 1

Searching for New Year

1st January to 29th January

"Without the blackbird, in whose throat the sweetness of the green fields dwells, the days would be only partly summer." - Richard Jefferies

A winter's chorus opened a grey day and the first day of January, but my New Year arrives when the blackbird returns to song after the silence of its summer moult, a silence that continues as days shorten, deep into winter. So each day I set out to find the return of the blackbird's voice. On this first day, I visited the heart of my local landscape of Needwood, where once a wild forest stood, but now just a few parcels of wood pasture remain between hedgerows and pastoral land. One such wood pasture is Brankley, a place I return to throughout the year, a landscape where solitude's spirit can be found in winter's mists, a summer woodland of hidden spaces, a place I struggle to leave as it reflects each season with intensity. On this January day at Brankley, a verve of clouds in blue was quickly extinguished by more threatening brethren, and the day became winter's grey, illuminated by the bright song of the robin. A band of rain passed, its frequency mapped out by sound with increasing intensity as it returned to land. A kestrel ripped down through the arriving stillness and disappeared into the grasses, emerging to depart with prey gripped between talons, as occasional breaks in the cloud appeared. Against a horizon looking like slate scree hewn from a Welsh mountain, a copse shone briefly in a flare of colour, before being returned to glorious gloom. Close by, below a deserted rookery, the robin was now plaintiff, as I set-off, climbing to a hilltop, where a blackbird sat silent, profiled below a waxing daytime moon.

The small woodland at Brook Hollows is my closest wood, a place I've known since childhood. A wood that became smaller as I grew, but has regrown as I've learnt how to see with the fascination of a child. I visit the hollows when I'd rather keep close to home, when time is tight, light is fading or the distant summer's heat discourages a longer walk. On this short winter's day, a week into January, I was drawn in again in my search for the blackbird's song. Alder cones, blown free by the gales, were scattered on the pathways, those rivers of human habit across the landscape. Spent birch slashed the bracken, a magpie lifted with sunshine wings and long-tailed tits navigated the strong air in low, short jumps. At a clearing in the heart of the wood, the buffeted trees seemed to be hanging on as the planet span, their high branches fluid as rooted trunks grasped the earth. I stood with them at ground level, where the air was calm and the chatter of birds could be heard, but the blackbird did not sing. There were many birds weaving the trees, and I let them be themselves and their patterns, rather than thinking of their labels. With the day closing, I looked down and noticed a trail of deer prints before me, they were small, from muntjac I thought, and I set-off to follow them; a pathway and habit shared.

I continued my search for New Year on the most beautiful of January days at Brankley Pasture, mild and bright with cloud teased across the blue. There was a fusion of birdsong and robins echoed one another; one climbing ever higher on its chosen branch as a blackbird perched silent beyond. The blackbird also seemed to listen, for when the robin left it did not sing to fill the void and announce New Year, it departed too. I passed a kestrel sat hooded grim, a peregrine, the pale and upright executioner, and a dozen black coots in the January stillness. A pair of crows explored the naked oak and fifty lapwings, broad and dichotomous, left the field as I crossed towards the trees. There, plumed seeds of the rosebay willowherb were silver sentinel ghosts in the gloom of the wood, arched over the path like a sabre arch at a woodland wedding. Trees weakened by honey fungus had succumbed to the wind and pigeon remains were scattered in the woodland ride, where the bats occupy the night.

Days later and there was a silence of snow at Brankley. It formed smooth sinusoidal arcs over clumps of grasses in the rough pasture. I imagined the mounds as the emerging heads of an underground army, buried upright to guard the trees; entwined by their roots in the cold brown earth, waiting to be fed by the fallen and decaying snag trees. The midday sun had been reduced by the deadweight of January sky, but by the evening, its talons scoured the horizon, the trail of a departing phoenix defeated by the stillness of the day. It was a stillness that encased the landscape and held all within, impervious to the blackbird that hammered with alarm at the dusk, like a flighted blacksmith, trapped behind a window on the world, mute of song and denied the freedom of the air and dalliance of space by the blanket of silence.

Back near my home, between Brook Hollows and the rookery wood, I walked yesterday's snow across the meadow, where the tops of individual grasses were a thousand trails in the expanse of white; some other sky of comets in some other world where matter has coalesced about a star. It was a breezy day, but towards the north west corner of this field is a place often still of wind, where one can stand and hear the blown canopy bellow as the wind tells its secrets to the leaves. Yet out in the open, where one has to be determined against the gale, the beat of the great tit still won free from the roar of the hollows. I reached rookery wood, where drifts of snow revealed the secret patterns and shape of the wind, a channel in the lee of a trunk showing where one day it might fall.

Toward the end of the day, as I walked towards my home through the cooling night air, the low moon travelled with me, shy beyond the copse. It focussed a sphere of attention on each tree that passed, revealing an ever-changing fractal network of darkness. The moon's glow permeated the surrounding cloud as if it had descended into our atmosphere. And I thought of other orbs of light, the kingfisher and departing magpie, the perfection of the snowberry; how nature can be smooth or angular, but always of compelling beauty. The cold on my bare hands returned me to reality, as the quarter peel of the church bells, rather than the blackbird's song, crossed the village to signal day's end.

A few days later I headed to the edge of the parish, where counties meet along the River Dove and the blackbird might sing. This is a place I had discovered the previous September, when I repeated my first visit on six consecutive days as I sought familiarity. On those first trips, I was fascinated by the river, cradled by the landscape as it carried the spirit of its upland source to the flatlands of the meadows. It offered new sounds, the return of leaping fish, calm rapids with countless voices, like audible leaves on a tree. And by the river, lies a clear oxbow lake, where the shadows of willows reach over the flat fields for the flow of the river beyond. Dragonflies course above the water lilies and the heron is always about. Over those consecutive trips, I visited at different times to read the various stories of the day. Especially that cusp of time between night and day, where haunting sounds precede the emergence of swans in flight as they appear from the half-light, spectral white shaded to reveal form against the grey. On this January day by the Dove, the colour of the alder, spirit of the ash and static vigour of the hawthorn circuited the oxbow and all seemed content to rest as I watched the dance of the willow. The stillness of the water allowed me to look down, yet up through its wonder of movement. Close-by, the tree I'd named the painter's alder leant over the oxbow, forever reaching for its own reflection. Its trunk was bright and curved as the neck of the swan that swam below; every angle explored in its balance, as it paused on the bank like winter's time.

The pause of nature during winter stretches the wait for the blackbird's New Year, but a cutting crystal frost at dawn released another day and I spent the morning by the oxbow once more. Nature had worked a transformation. Every natural form had a new layer that engaged the light and transformed the ordinary. My progress rotated the painter's alder through all its forms to silhouette as it turned about its axis. The flat and frosted floodplain was intense in the sunlight, a white dusted sea of green led to the river that flowed cheerfully alongside crystallised brethren, yet a passing kingfisher managed to amplify even this intensity of light. It was a day to walk and write on foot, enjoying the time as the bright landscape seemed to anticipate the blackbird's coming song.

I continued upstream for a little while, on the bank between hawthorn and willow, following the curves to where the shallows can be heard. I arrived at the remains of the quarter-mile bridge, where steam trains once crossed the river. A concrete pillbox sat alien and square. Imposed and descended. Cutting and heavy. Deliberate and forlorn. The cell of connectedness for those without the sense for nature, those deaf to the song of the Earth. Where humans had carved the landscape, through railway embankments, flood defences and remains of ridge and furrow, the contours perpendicular to the sun were green. The frost now liquid drops, clinging to the grass, green waves running across the dusted sea. I continued my voyage towards my New Year, past grasses sugared by frost and paper cut hogweed that stood proud of the remaining herbage of summer. Longer grasses curled, like fibre optic arcs, white cloud chamber traces of particles in some quantum world. A bullfinch guarded a bank-side willow as the River Dove looked to boil, distant ripples bouncing the sun. Mist rose above the water and a young alder rained against the sun, this day was a scene of joy.

That afternoon I travelled to another of my regular haunts at Dunstall, a place of mature woodland and new plantations on the Trent valley risings, where I could stand until only the landscape remained. A place so familiar to me that I can walk it within my mind's eye and sense the changes in the feel of the air as it finds channels through the landscape. By the afternoon, the sun that challenged my eyes had vanished vast tracts of frost, but much remained in the shadows of the woods where the robin sang loud. Through the bracken, I entered the heart of the wood and found myself in a bright clearing, between the evergreen cherry laurels shooting green. Beyond the woodland, frosted paths chalked through the long grasses, sunken from the sun.

The sun set with frost still in the shade. Silent blackbirds flew direct into the fading light and rooks were in flight about their nests. I imagined their higher perspective of the landscape and let my mind soar with them, together seeing more as we toured above the woodland canopy and lines of the plantations that pattern the slopes. I returned to earth and walked as the sun's fall produced a wider brightness in the sky. At the lake, air was trapped beneath ice like white leaves of a water lily. A grey wagtail departed, dark against the sun. Present and of the landscape, nature was my thoughts and they were the networked pathways of the trees, asking how a tree supported stoutly, divides to nothing.

How the path of a bird is invisible in the air it disturbs. How the unseen is no less real. How mind might be as it extends beyond our bodies to bring the landscape inside.

A robin's song tried to explain as it shared the patterns of my mind. I could feel it, like a gentle hook on my consciousness, that wrapper of thought and being that engulfs the activity of which we are unconscious. How song and shape arrives without our knowing. This hook of robin's song seemed to be other than sound, a connection not through the senses, but as if as one, such was my place in the landscape at that moment. The song was my sound, reflected my mind and the fading warmth of the sun was the warmth of my blood, for our flesh is inseparable from the flesh of the Earth. I had realised this months before after spending a year writing as I walked. Making simple notes of my interactions with the natural world, the stimuli I noticed within it and my response. This was not a dry scientific account, but writing that grew from attentive observation and documentation to a lyrical celebration of the joys of finding deep nature in the local countryside. Ultimately, it changed my understanding of my *self* and its shared place in the landscape. I progressed from observer of the natural world to an emotional connectedness manifested in a greater appreciation of the beauty and energy of the landscape. At first, I saw little more than nature's details, but with repeated engagement and time, a different landscape was revealed. I increasingly felt part of nature, I started to refer to the flesh of the Earth, flowed through nature's veins as I walked and felt the landscape and my mind merge, my sense of self dissolve. I started to realise that the natural world and landscape is not an external *Other*, something we encounter – it is part of our being.

This is the story of my continued journey through the flesh of the Earth, bounded by the blackbird's year, considering our embeddedness in the natural landscape and the nature of mind along the way. Observing the story of the day, ties one into it, to be part of the patterns of nature, rather than the pursuit of linear goals. By being immersed in the landscape away from intrusive thoughts, a place can be found in the present moment, where nature can be experienced in an open and accepting way. A systematic engagement with nature, achieved through writing on foot, leads to a deep knowing and freedom of mind that enhances the sensory impact of nature still further.

January was progressing and the blackbird was still silent. Its hidden song the essence of spring imbibed within its blackness. A melody enclosed and waiting to be released each dawn until summer is established and the blackbird can moult in silence once more. I set out, hoping to hear the catalyst of spring. Walking the pathways about my home I saw a hollow based oak, alone and agape at the gales, its inners plunged by the sun's light. Surrounding hedgerows leant towards the nearby pool where more trees stood firm. Their green trunks, slender against the blue, reaching upward and swaying as moss clung to their base. I stood surrounded by the suspended brightness of the reed heads, curving to the wind, never still, ever changing, always reeds. Dropped branches blocked my path and displayed their lichen to new eyes, and beyond the lane sank away. Fallen crab apples and fungi spotted the verge, bright circular forms random amongst the faded lines of summer. These images and sounds, scents and textures are both nature and mind. The fluency of nature flows with effortless abandon, consumed by our senses to be known, to become familiar, to become part of our being and self.

I continued across barren fields, another place of mind, towards Brook Hollows, arriving first at rookery wood. Here the wind ripped through, ash saplings shook and grasses were wrenched and tugged. Fallen branches shorn of bark lay, white snakes twisting through the undergrowth, chasing leaves, which panicked away, as a herd of mice might, heading for cover, only for some to be caught and hung on the barbed wire. The willow nearby was live, lithe and bold of hue, as a buzzard, harassed by two rooks, tamed the gales to evade, circle and hang, bright and of easy form, flexing yet stable.

The next day, at Brankley, I saw the woods as one. One barred mass within the green pasture, each tree lined further by the shadows of those before. Bending to the wind as one, slender silvered trunks of beech curved the air, their branches reaching upwards, darker and more sinuous as they divided into ever-thinner versions of what went before. I leant against a tree to shelter from the gale, to feel the warmth of the sun and to let my mind wander through the landscape. In the wind, leaves became flocks of finches in flight across the fields to the hedgerow. All the time I was gently rocked back and forth by the tree that was my support, its underlying strength apparent. Gently swayed, I felt I should climb the tree higher and be at sea, riding its stationary voyage through the waves of the wind. On through the ocean of mind I went, seeing redwings departing and a warning of crows, at any moment one of these trees could fall. I turned to face the wind and rode the channel to open ground.

As the month neared its end I returned to the oxbow, where the sun's light scoured the bare landscape. It turned all to brightness and shade, revealing all forms and casting dimensions into shadow for my mind to give meaning, to become place. From within the reflected sun, the swans appeared as black as the neighbouring coot and the black masses of the rooks about their nests; the only white was the spiralling primaries of the departing magpie. I accepted the surroundings, attending to them for what they might bring, the new thinking they might become. What had been riverbank had collapsed to become the shallow bed of the swollen river, its grasses unwillingly indicating the flow and jinking the light with hanging drops where they broke the surface. I inspected the far bank, trying to catch sight of the bullfinch that chattered amongst a fallen shrub laid along its steep sides; showing where the Dove had flowed high. All the time the river slipped by, doubling the sun and gently singing to me through the air.

On the near bank, a line of flotsam marked the river's maximum extent, molehills were smoothed and iridescent cirrostratus cloud gave winter colour. Stood, looking out over the flatness, the power of the landscape was palpable to me. Whereas the coast has the energy of sound and crashing movement, the flatlands have seen all that. The pebbles that lie upon the turned earth hold their form as testament to eons of energy coursing the landscape; and there it resides, seeping out to those that stand still and see.

Returning home, there was white in the hollows: white bells of the snowdrops shivered as they captured the movement of what seemed still air. They were based by stunted, blunt blades with a light tip, and grouped like footprints across the woodland floor. I stood still, woven by the birdsong into the calm of the hollows, sensing the proximity of the trees about me. Returning, my footsteps shone where they had leeched moisture to the surface of the compressed leaf mould, shining like the trail of the clustered snowdrops.

A few days later, the frosts seemed to have frozen both space and time and the day lay still on the flatlands by the River Dove as I set out on a straight, level walk. The silence screamed of the nadir of winter, spring must appear soon. Above the frozen mists, a skylark wound the vapours and a crow stirred the air, its blackness being all that was solid. The trees that dress the landscape sat indistinct as, in the distance, from deep within the pit of silence, a blackbird's song engraved itself on the icy air, as the day lay done. It was New Year.

Chapter 2

Mind and Nature

30th January to 25th February

"The mind joys in the knowledge that it too is a part of this wonder—akin to the ten thousand thousand creatures, akin to the very earth itself." - Richard Jefferies

As I passed the painter's alder by the Dove, the sun lay its beam across the plain and I walked along its unfurled glory. A blackbird left against the sun, the wing filtered light like a burst of song. The coot departed the arched, sunken willow to the far bank as waves of audible ripples navigated the breeze. The eroded banks dropped sharply, edging and containing the flow. I stood and watched the Dove ripple away, left then right until out of sight, as the light bounced the surface. The trees beyond were all bare, bar the January purple of the alder against the spent tones of grasses, and the lichened green of the willow trunks supporting gold twigs above. As I walked alongside the river, puddles in the track-way reflected blue, giving a still perspective to the extent of mind as they converged away.

There seemed to be a symbiosis between the brightness of day and the bright beat of the birdsong. The brown Dove eddied, its surface a two dimensional universe of flat, rotating galaxies. Their motion through space-time described by the physics that describe all matter, together with the processes and relationships that govern us and embed us into the natural landscape – real despite having no matter. Yet, to understand our place in nature more fully one needs to think about mind, that non-matter often placed inside our heads, but that we know little about.

For me, writing on foot in the local landscape, describing the joy of shared nature, is also thinking about the process that is mind. The act of writing is not simply an output of thought, a substitute for speech or recording of knowledge: writing enables and shapes our thinking. Sentences carry thought and help create new thinking, so writing in nature also develops our thinking about our relationship to nature. This is true of classic writing such as Nan Shepherd's *The Living Mountain* where, without recognition, Shepherd demonstrated new thinking in line with that of the philosopher Merleau-Ponty.

From the opening page of *The Living Mountain*, Shepherd tackled mind head on, all of the reality that matters to us, is a reality of mind, that non-matter which is our every conscious moment, an impenetrable graphene conducting the only thoughts we ever know, but which cannot carry the landscape away – hence our need to return, again and again to understand it. The book is a phenomenology, a study of consciousness and lived experience that takes place on the mountain and captures the very act of being. How the body is our own instrument of discovery, that can be fettled and tuned to see the depth of being, like a telescope can see a deep field view of the Universe, yet neither is ever fully understood. Lying on the mountain, in that place between insentience and alertness, Shepherd found an uncompromised connection with the earth where the mind holds a flame of nature into the depth of slumber and becomes uncoupled, the sense of self and familiarity of place dissolves, such that the mind is a void until one awakes and is human once more. Shepherd joins the realities of self and nature and joys in the perception of the world, each sense a route into what nature has to give, channels of existence in the natural world such that mind can impregnate matter and create a living spirit that can walk out of the body and into the landscape.

As I stood by the River Dove, a direct experience of mind in nature, I considered the earlier and classic nature writers who have trod the pathways of mind before me. During the 1850s, in books such as *Walden* and *Walking*, Henry Thoreau considered the impact of nature upon mind, but there was little deep thought into the nature of mind. In the 1836 essay, *Nature*, Ralph Waldo Emerson wrote of the flow of nature into mind and its impact, but again tends not to consider the nature of mind beyond writing "the whole of nature is a metaphor of the human mind". I found that it was Richard Jefferies who explored that landscape of mind, finding his own eddies in the river, as I saw before me, spiralling the current in the Dove.

As I follow these footsteps in my local landscape I have felt an affinity with Jefferies' joy at finding intensity in everyday nature. His awareness stepped beyond that of the seen and heard with an explosion of reference to mind from late 1882. In the article *The Sun and the Brook*, Jefferies' lyrical writing extended the flesh into the landscape and, like Shepherd, showed a thinking that has similarities to the mid-twentieth century philosophy of Merleau-Ponty. Merleau-Ponty wrote of "the Flesh" as a collective term for the flesh of the human body and the flesh of the world and highlighted the interconnection between the perceived and perceiver – we are embedded in the landscape.

"The grass sways and fans the reposing mind; the leaves sway and stroke it, till it can feel beyond itself and with them, using each grass blade, each leaf, to abstract life from earth and ether. These then become new organs, fresh nerves and veins running afar out into the field, along the winding brook, up through the leaves, bringing a larger existence. The arms of the mind open wide to the broad sky."

Richard Jefferies, The Sun and the Brook

Throughout work published in 1883 Jefferies considered mind with great regularity. He contemplated the interaction of mind and nature, the need of mind for nature and extended the mind into the landscape. He discussed the elusive mind, free of laws that rule matter, the power of mind, and the untapped mind that no thought has sailed. Although, in *The Story of My Heart*, Jefferies still appears to view nature as separate, referring to the repellent toad, creatures that shock the mind such that by no reasoning can nature be fitted to mind.

Yet, repeated journeys through the local landscape, noting nature and writing on foot can reveal the unity of mind and nature. By 1884 Jefferies writes of the "sweet accordance" of mind and nature, how it is "absorbed by beauty"; a choice of words that suggests an interconnectedness. And as his mind wandered "deeper and farther into the dreamy mystery of the azure sky", Jefferies wrote of unknown grand thoughts "hovering as a swallow above". Finally, in *Nature and Eternity*, published posthumously in May 1895, Jefferies writes:

"We are of the great community of living beings, indissolubly connected with them from the lowest to the highest by a thousand ties."

This development of thinking through repeatedly walking the local pathways continues into his final works such as *The Open Air*, where in 1885, he considered mind being made happy by unconscious visceral experience of nature, rather than reflection – an idea with similarities to more recent thinking on the different levels of brain mechanism, pre-reflective processing and perceptual fluency. In *The Open Air*, Jefferies also touches on issues considered by modern day thinkers. He writes of the abstraction of the written word, how "in the mind all things are written in pictures – there is no alphabetical combinations of letters and words". And how oral learning of nature in the landscape takes "root in the mind" much sooner than abstract presentation in books. More recently, the American philosopher David Abram has written of how the abstract symbolism of the written word, and loss of oral learning in the landscape to learning from texts, has played a part in the human disconnection with nature. And all this is why I take these simple journeys of discovery, noting nature and searching for wilderness in the local landscape, by listening to the spiralling stories carried by the River Dove or resting in Brook Hollows.

My experience of writing in nature has compelled me to consider our place as biological beings in the landscape and what we share with nature. We only understand the natural world and the local landscape of stream and copse because our minds and bodies are embedded within it, so that we live with and through the environment around us. Just as hand tools are integrated by the mind into the schemata of the body, the material and natural world beyond are deeply integrated into our experience. This is because our brains did not evolve to think, they came about in order to make sense of the world around us, so that we could better survive. And our body, as described by Merleau-Ponty, is "the vehicle of being in the world". And our mind is born with that body, but lives between it and the Earth, yet we can never walk far enough away to see it, as that walking is the activity, the sensing, the being, that is mind. Our senses secure access to the world and are how we explore it; we are all explorers of the landscape each time we stand still within it. Each bird, each song, and each part of the landscape we see, hear and sense, our shared interaction in the landscape is mind: it is not inside our heads. So to understand mind we are better to understand our place in the landscape, the landscape we evolved to fit and explore. Such that knowing our place, is knowing our *self*.

We are our mind, and our mind is our activity, being and place in the landscape. Move, and we are changed; the shepherd cannot be a shepherd in the forest, and a person in the city is different to that same person in the countryside. Each location, each place, has a geology and geography that leads to a certain habitat, flora and fauna that creates the local atmosphere and place of mind; be it a region, valley or nook between rocks by a stream. We return to our favourite mindscapes as they disappear when we leave; no image, no writing, no neurone of memory can truly capture place.

So I return again and again to the woods and riverbanks, but I am not searching for the boundaries of self where it meets external nature. Nor do I explore my limits by confronting the natural world to become more aware of its otherness. Rather, I realise my place in the natural world by finding what is shared, by being of it. There are no boundaries, our minds and our very being is embedded within the natural world. A resurgence in the thinking of others on life and mind, extended mind and the biology of consciousness makes this shared place excitingly real.

I set out to Brook Hollows, writing on foot, thinking nature, and looking for a reflection of mind. Within the depth of winter, on the greyest and wettest of days, when black trees seem to seep into the grey there is wonder; wonder in the charge of the single drop of chilled rain on the face as it actions the body at the interface; chemical and electric potentials change this physical reality into that non-matter of mind. We know its place and can hold that instant of sensation as a ripple on the film of consciousness that is the surface of the pool of mind. Also rippling the pool were the sights and sounds. Where photons become other and ripples in the air vibrate through ossicle and incus to take new form. And I knew that without sense there is no landscape. Like mists, the mind explores the landscape through the senses that gather that which describes it. The sounds of the winds shaped by the land and trees, stitched by the birds into a tapestry that the ears can read. The light reflected by hill, oak and stream; photons from space gathered within the eye to prick out an image on a mind's eye.

As I returned from Brook Hollows, the indigo of night inked the sky, cloud lay flat on the western horizon as Jupiter kept the moon close and Venus was as sharp as the air. The dark, freezing dry air grips, as does the humid air of August; both make themselves known, one keen, the other slovenly, willing to bring discomfort to the interface of our skin, where body makes sense of wider nature. I retreated indoors and read the mirror of mind in the trail of words, footprints of the day.

The following day, the kingfisher ignited a routine sub-zero morning. From its willow perch above the ford in the village, it dropped like Mother Nature's own tear, all of nature's colour falling to the water to emerge as a bird, and it returned to its perch to dive once more. Sometimes nature does so much more than suggest a place to pause, it shouts and forces one to stand. And once divorced from the activities of the day, nature has time to tell its story. And the story that morning continued, a blackbird against the frost, wings and primaries outstretched to translucent as it cleared the winter's hawthorn. The beat of a woodpecker nailed my mind and the kingfisher passed once more. Where the water was still, it was frozen metallic, crazed and pitted with imprints of the swan. Beneath the ice, the water was fluid and from the edge it exited free to re-join the flow.

The next morning, I continued my perpetual search for the unknown grand thoughts Jefferies had sensed hovering above, those that can only be found by open, pre-reflective attention; whose fragments arrive after weeks of repetition. By the oxbow, individual flakes of white, that might be snow, speckled the hard, frost-dried earth. A buzzard passed, its plumage a mirror of the snow-dusted earth beneath and a kingfisher drew its colour long, signing the darkness of the water. A lone crow balanced the willow from its perch and the freezing dry air carried its sound. A great spotted woodpecker, shot red, passed, patterned flight audible. The iced hues of the oxbow were gentle under the cutting air. A shockwave was trapped on the surface of the frozen water, it arced from the base of the painter's alder and stopped at the point its hanging branches touched the water. The trees and grasses were as still as the ice that dealt the suns rays into fragments, and the chattering of the unseen seemed to give voice to the trembling leaves, dried and forgotten by Autumn. Birdsong was the only time, the only sign that the Earth had not stopped turning.

I had enjoyed the morning blue above the frost, but how a day can change. The cloud came and having travelled to the Derbyshire peaks, I felt the tearing cold of the wind on White Edge, the stark beauty of lifeless forms, stream side grasses weighted by icicles, bowed like rods landing a big catch. The snow covered hills were Wainwright sketches pricked out of a page of sky, points of blackness defining their features and extent. Then came a return to the valley and the silence of the snow, ghosted by the wind, still within the trees. A pool of contrasts, ice-free black, snow dusted solid white and that grey that lies in-between. Loaded reeds and bulrushes taken to white. Trees with white relief from clinging flakes that spelt out each branch; white topped, creeping across my vision as glossy ink running down a page. Crossing, reaching, ending in brittle forms. Cracks in a frosted pane, making the diverse complexity bold. And the flat dark pool reflected it so well. To the fore, a long fallen willow's growth reached skyward. Vertical, unmarked by the snow, merging with distant trees. Standing there, I was marked by the snow and my mind was calmed.

The tracked snow about me compressed time, an external memory, recording the habits of that which rides the landscape. I followed the fox close to field boundaries and over walls, rabbits and the six-foot leaps of the hare. The birch on the valley side were their own mist, tumbling waves of frosted purples and greys. Then a thought hovered down from the low clouds and it struck me, the transformational wonder of snow is akin to the joy of seeing a familiar landscape with mindful eyes. The landscape can be changed through our perspective: it's not the landscape that matters, but the way we view it, the mindscape.

I returned home to another bright morning by the oxbow, the cold wind was as sharp as the light and where there was shadow the earth was firm. Here, remaining frosts caught what light there was and the sound underfoot became crisp, digital compared to the analogue of sodden soils, but the heron's character remained constant. It became apparent as it lifted from tired reeds and I watched as its wings embraced the air. Like the heron, a grey wagtail appeared as it took flight from the pebbles, as if it had changed state from stone to flesh and wing. The river was also two, flowing with liquid dynamic and lit crests about fallen banks; yet a solid and silent body at its centre, like flowing earth with broad arced ripples seemingly holding constant position; creating a smile of reflected sky. As I returned along the river bank, the last leaves of a young oak flew to become blue tits and I considered how things can be two: hard earth and soft, light and shade, moving or still, apparent or not, pebble or bird, mind or matter. And I realised once again how much there is in the winter landscape, especially for fallible eyes.

I walked on and crossed the river and county border to a place where the ruins of Tutbury Castle stand as crags on a landscape that rises from the wide valley floor. Retreating floodwaters revealed an old watercourse in the flatlands. As I looked it seemed to moat a distant spire as it curved within ancient contours refound; recapturing and dividing the land, revealing undulations in the flatness. A line of flotsam, the wreckage of seasons past, drew a new level on the banked earth of the flood defence. Weaves of patterned thatch giving the impression of a roof on a long house, topped by a shuttlecock and a sandal, plastic in the expanse of nature.

The landscape was at its most bare and bleak, where I could become the flesh to its bones and find deep nature. The merest glow of spent life was lifted by the smallest signs of spring; the catkins budding on the willow, spotted white notes of a blackbird's song. Cold. Stillness. But the river always carries the season on. Two-dozen rooks perched on a wire beat out a rhythm of coming spring. And through days of bleakness, when the rhythm seemed lost, brightness arrived as it would. A drawn bright sky set the oak's divisions apparent, against bands of opposing colours. Birdsong needled the grooves that wrapped the sky dome, and a blackbird's alarm jumped; repeating the same note until danger passed. The fire of sun lit the spinney as the air cooled the flesh. In the dusk of the hollows, branches were dark serpents in the water as blackbirds shot low, calls following like tracer, audio pyrotechnics bright in the ear. And as the light faded the woods became a denser flesh, pulsing with the signals of a return to night. Two rooks in flight balanced about Jupiter, their shapes evolving, expanding and contracting through all of their forms about the first point of light in the dome. I was charged and ready for a new mindscape where new thoughts hover.

Field mists halved the trees and landscape was lost beneath a clear moon as I headed south to Devon, past nineteen buzzards and a black fox on the Somerset levels.

The coast at the mouth of the Otter had the feeling of the end of the Earth, a lost chunk of time and space, a piece of planet where fossils were laid down. Coast, a place to end one journey or begin another, and I knew this place would take my mind and weave it with the air, water and earth. There was a milky light and greys of stone. An air of seaweed on the breeze and the river flowed silver where the red cliffs stopped. The pines beyond were cut by passing gulls. The sea was a flat, rolling mass, patterned by ripples and calm, lined by brightness on the horizon due south. Dozens more gulls headed that way, low, riding their reflection. Hard rounded pebbles shrank into the mist with the headland beyond. Each pebble its own shape, size and colour; rich and lustred when wet, matt and pallid when not. They lay as they do, piled above a glimpsed darkness beneath. Receiving what comes, solid and still, on a small sand bank before me, isolated by the tide. The out flowing river raced towards it, but veered away to become the sea. The tide slipped away and I remained, no longer an island.

Inland, the sun lit a complex tree to yellow. Its twisting branches and clusters of bud bearing twigs were clear and further delineated by lichen forms, the whole mass appeared as a neural network. This mind was occupied by brightness, goldfinches, robin and a bullfinch bold; blackbird, blue tit, great and coal. Each bird a thought, idea or memory, connected by looping flights, to other minds in a shared cognition. Roots embedded the thinking flesh into the earth. Separate, but as one were the perceiver and the perceived. I felt my trunk become solid, my limbs stiffened. I could feel the sinews within, channelling and supporting. There was no vision, no movement, just calm existence. Then I was the jackdaw gliding to its perch. Quill of feathers entered my flesh and as I drifted, I could see the land below turning to night and I slept as bird or man.

First light, and the sky reflected the stillness with a smooth progression of pink to grey, and return. Birdsong filled every moment of the calm. From raucous rooks to the sweet trill of the goldfinch, the tree was busy. I searched for one moment of silence within the chatter, but each time the song from those close-by subsided the distant backing filled time and the depth of the sound was revealed; like a deep field view of the cosmos where blackness always has a hidden star. I closed my eyes and floated out into it, amongst the tide of corvid cries to be swayed by the breaking and rolling crests of the collard dove. Each wavelet and sparkling reflection picked out by the call of others. I was carried out by the current until my mind was only waves of blue. After sometime the intensity of the birdsong started to subside and I emerged where I started, under the tree.

It was time to walk, to find the unforeseen thoughts that arrive as they will, like the coming of the blackbirds return to song. The Devon lane snaked away from the tree, and I followed it deep between banked hedgerows, sided by a clear streamlet. A large oak straddled the bank and others picked out the route. Drifts of snowdrops fell; primroses and cowslips dared speak of spring as the robin's song lost its plaintiff air. Silver trunks of beech caged the bank, multiple stems rising from moss and tongues of fernage, as the stream ran free past a window on the woods. The banked earth had been eroded and undercut to reveal the roots within, now grasping air to stay grounded as a heron embraces it to fly. At the base of the lane, where routes met, water pooled. Crows rose and the dropping light described the oaks dimensions, and I felt that I saw time. The skies were clearing and I turned to face times light and saw the far hills recede into bright mists, the beat of the landscape, its breath through the trees, hanging mists that made the birch trees seem even more delicate. A bevy of long tailed tits cracked and popped in the young oak above me. Casting a dark shadow against the bark of the oak, kindly lit by the sun on a pure February day: blue, crisp and everything edged by the brightness. A tall slender beech was shadowed with elegant curves by a neighbour. They swept upwards in compelling form to make this one tree stand out from the many. I felt replenished, ready to wake from a reality that felt like a dream.

Back home, where the flat landscape about the Dove releases the energy of lost form, a stumped willow exploded with twiggy growth; an explosion intensified by the canvas of sparkling light provided by the oxbow behind. It was a day of bright life, an unlikely light of the dried reeds and welcome warmth on a breeze that set all in motion. I felt thrilled to be at the oxbow with the feeling of spring. Even the dry, lifeless cones of the budding alder could not temper as they rocked in unison with their supporting branch. The embroidered catkins of the hazel, in triples and twos, seemed content as a skylark flooded the plain, each note playing with every blade of grass, before being diminished and lost on the wind. I envisioned the exchange between my body and the Earth as I made peaceful progress. My mind flooded the space of the plain as the river floods it, lying calm, rippling and washing; mind as landscape. The birdsong mined my memories of summer, I could hear the blackbird's year ahead and see it in the high clouds. I stood on each mound of higher ground hoping to reach towards grand thoughts carried high on the breeze. I drew on a deep pit of joy and anticipation and vowed to find a place of unity within the stories of nature.

The following day I explored new pathways through the heart of Needwood and found a place where the light revealed the depth of the wood. Hanging dendrites of pine above golden memories of fern. Columns of thought, ideas, a vision. Like the body, the wood passed its boundary; leaves scattered the fields as shadow blocked the path of the sun. The reaching, branching and reducing growth of the trees became the air itself and the birdsong from within escaped through that air to touch each surface beyond. The wood was good.

At the woodland's edge, the nuthatch rang and redwing sang, six buzzards paired the sky; patterned, authoritative, aloft with graced ease. A skylark flowed sound and rose to bullet down on another. Hollies rippled with light, a galaxy of bright stars around the darkness of the leant oak, its form as a candle melting in time. As I arrived at a roadside, crazy horses travelled by. As we extend our occupation of nature, we reduce nature's occupation of our minds. Indebted to the price of land, forgetting the value it gives for free.

Looking up, not along, exploring further, I found a new alder, contorted with time through space as it explored the air above the stream. Sunlight, channelled by branches, lined the last of the morning's mist to light the ripples and a robin was at pleasure. Such was the joy I retraced my steps to see the alder again on its sunny side, where the stream turned obstructions into a melody as constant and bright as the rippled reflections on my trunk. A buzzard planed above the copse and my day was done.

February came towards a close with the blue skies of summer and I returned to the Dove. The blackbird brought an orb of calm, its blackness lit bright with a ring of orange circling a mind-feeding eye. Perched, sensing, there in the sun it was a being of the present moment, no more. The wren arrived and robin too, but it was the blackbird that was most composed, brought most calm before it dipped from view, to be replaced by a grand fieldfare that posed, defending a waterfall of berries.

I walked the river, its cut bank stood as a sandstone wall, draped with hanging grasses. What was always a ditch drained the field, its outflow launching over the trunk of a collapsing willow. Revealing and smoothing the clay beneath to a bowl of burnished bronze. Close by a dead swan lay, the second I'd found in recent weeks. A trail of feathers showed where it had been dragged from the water. Fleshless, its white spine and ribs were partnered by pointless wings.

Long shadows crossed the meadow, grass blades pointed with light. As I walked on, brightness projected my form into a small wood, through hedgerows, beyond paths, to undergrowth and climbing trees. Rapid, defined, at once, stretching out and touching; taking mind forth into nooks and crannies of the wood. Until I found a cathedral of mind, a clearing where a dozen trunks rose, pillars of thought beneath a canopy of green. A fresco that sounded out the rain, coloured the light and fell each autumn, leaving a skeleton of leaden branches to be renewed each spring. Standing there I wondered if the stuff of cosmos is less chance and more a system destined to generate life and mind. And each life is that cosmos waking, somehow, like a murmuration of starlings, aware of its path, yet dispersed through beings. After sometime with these grand thoughts I walked on, to where the shadows from two slender trunks lined a pathway and my shadowed form navigated in-between, deforming to be joined whenever it approached an edge, penumbras of life merging.

Chapter 3

Calling Rooks

29th February to 31st March

"The civilised rooks, with their libraries of knowledge in their old nests of reference." - Richard Jefferies

Sixteen rooks, paired and static, sat dark against a chalk dusted sky; red plumes of vapour clinging to a pastel blue. Below, the blackbirds were in full voice, their renewed vigour releasing spring. The waters of the hollows were silken in the dusk light; ripples broad, motion slowed. Birdcalls picked the cooling air as the western sky grew softer still, hazing the imprinted hedgerow trees, questioning my focus. On my return, the rooks were still bonded to their trees, as Jupiter, an arrowhead drawn by the hand of Venus, targeted the half-moon that rose above the lights of the land possessed.

The Victorian naturalist, Charles Waterton includes an essay on rooks in his 1837-1857 series of works published in 1871 as Essays on Natural History (my copy was originally presented to Frederick Rains as a special prize for religious knowledge, June 9th 1875). Waterton noted their regular daily movements, nesting, feeding and roosting in flocks throughout the year. How their flight during passage to the feeding grounds is dependent on the weather, skimming the tree tops in gales, flying high with a regular beat of the wing when it is calm. Observing that as the day nears an end, the rooks rise and circle for a while before heading to their roost.

As a naturalist, Waterton had an ecologistic and analytical relationship to the rook, whereas the more recent rook watcher Esther Woolfson, found the humanistic, naturalistic and aesthetic values that can be found in a connection to the rook. Her close contact led to an emotional attachment and appreciation of the beauty to be found in their gilded form and grace of stillness. Woolfson found a common world, realising what we share, from backbone and brain structures, to senses and social existence. Joined by pathways of evolution, biology and shared habit; pathways without boundary through a depth of time. Those that have not realised commonality with the rook can perceive harsh voices and fear dark forces of an under-world in the treetops; such that they are unaware of the rook's fears, affection and amusement. Judgements based on superstition and perceived otherness are at best a loss, at worse pernicious to others realisation of our shared place in the landscape. For me, when the rook bleeds its call my heart heals. Their voice skewers mind to the landscape. The hard rasp cutting a path that rides the cold air and the barbs tear mind and matter such that it weaves itself into a sense of place and being that affords a deep knowing of connection.

As February closed, March rose from the mists to engulf the Dunstall landscape and mind in spring. Wrapped in this place by time passed, I could have arrived by time machine. The earth of the bridleway moulded to each step, firm and accepting as the flesh of kin; an unquestioning direct bond. Numerous strands of gossamer web trailed from the hedgerow, horizontal before me, revealed by the light like a slow motion rain. The stark trees were compelling in their winter form, black against the bright sky, but I could sense the welling eruption of spring. Below the daytime moon, a pair of great spotted woodpeckers chased by to be balanced, vertical on the high branches. A flushed pheasant sent squirrels scattering, bringing drama to the woods and I completed the circuit content, deep in nature.

I set out each day, always passing the rookery close to home. In the hollows, moss lime trunks rose and fell through the leaf mould, weird serpents of the wood; a reflection of mind seen in folklore. In the grey of rain this forgotten corner drew me in, like the mosses absorbing the rain I soaked amongst the undergrowth. The sky cleared almost as rapid as an eye opens, watching me in the clearing, by the furred willow, bright to eyes and touch. Last year's leaves lay tarnished to black. Fungi layered the southern aspect of a fallen and rotting willow, like arcs of flint naps hammered into the bark. I looked down the tunnel of illuminated ash and arching willow, hanging drops on the horizontal growth patterned the route.

Balanced calls of great tits see-sawed through the trees as I sought the present moment and the exchange. The shaggy rook nests soared as the sun left rookery wood with winter's gloom. The alder bloomed, red felt tips of cones forming as close by blackbirds kept to ground or hedgerow. Long tailed tits lollipoped by as rain returned to be cupped by clover, droplets white as the sun shone. The angled light left the cloud and combed the meadow as if feeling its texture, sensing and bringing about mind-light.

Rooks marked the passage of time, black shards in space, salient forms on salient trees. A single bare oak with nest bore many birds and the earth below popped as it absorbed the recent rain.

The breeze about the replenished pond described the reeds and they spoke in return. As did the skylark and landscape itself, utterances of the wind, shaped by hills and trees, each point on the hillside having something to say. The faint ticking of birch as the bogged willow sank silently. I remained quietly present, passive to the wind and little appeared living bar the engaging forms of catkins and furred buds of willow. As the breeze dropped, there was calm and the birdsong came forth. Jaunty finches rose and lifted my gaze. The sky was as static as the air and I felt sensed by the landscape, mind in mind.

The following day I returned to Dunstall and was dealt winter's cards; spring retreated and after the rain the land sat engorged. I received the cold and looked out at slate grey cloud, rain and wind intersecting as a tanker of cloud crossed the western brightness. It was increasingly cold and murky, and seeking shelter I stood on the grasping knuckles at the base of the mighty beech as hail swept across. The pellets of ice started to fall vertically before the onslaught came to an end. Close by, the branches of a young beech reached out, soaked to black, barring the path; crisp gold-leaf hanging beyond silver lenses.

That night the landscape fell silent, no utterance human or animal, no rain or disturbance of air. The silence stretched until it was fractured by the song of dawn's robin, germinating in an instant and rapidly climbing the air into a rambling rose with blooms the orange of the robin's breast.

The awakening morning destroyed the rose of song and I sought out and explored a woodland at Calke Abbey. Skeleton leaves mapped their structure like satellite images of heart shaped cities, in a wood bereft of green. Fallen branches were blanched, grounded leaves faded through tans to white and with the pearled cloud above and the firmament of birch surrounding, the wood was a heaven. Rooks peppered the roof of this world and mind heard the sound of a dying witch coming from a tree swaying in the breeze. A breeze that was a serpent moving in the undergrowth, and also its breath. A fallen birch had rotted to bark, appearing like the shedded skin of the serpent of the wood; or serpent of the mind.

I spent that evening by the Dove. The low sun washed the river with gold and revealed how the meadow lay, each blade of grass sharp when lit.

The shadows of ash cast long, reaching towards the ploughed earth beyond. I felt summer in the light, winter in the wind and spring in the firm earth beneath my feet. The light gave the trees a depth of form and their varying tones stepped across the plain, the light of the budding willow, the alder too dark and matt to take the suns colour. Then the light was trapped and the magic was lost. The river flowed on as the season and I moved too, between the close circle of ash that gripped the land tight and I felt that there was to be no letting go. I could sense the purpose and steady power of their roots reaching into the soil. And then the kingfisher, I tracked its perch and watched it fly west where its light re-joined the orange sun, visible between passing clouds.

Days later and the landscape by the Dove was tulle veiled by risen March mists. Trees sat like creeping vapours and only the magpie close by was bold. The sun was a bright hole in the sky as winter's cold air and spring's sounds juxtaposed. Little of last summer was left standing, but less had risen to take its place. The swans left the meadow to join the oxbow and gain more elegant motion. As smooth as the misted air, they rode the reflections of the now present sun as a skylark lifted to speak of spring, its speck floating against the blue, its accelerated song seeming to slow surrounding time. The sound faded like the sun in the mists and the silence was prominent. The water beneath the painter's alder sparkled intensely, as the tree remained shadow upon shadow of the hedgerow beyond. As the sun withdrew once more the wind sought my flesh, drawing my warmth and sharing it with the landscape. Breezed rain showered the far land and the reeds had a stillness that befitted their pale colour. Birds made calm passage above teasels that gently rocked and the water had a depth of grey that exceeded the sky. Its stillness was compelling and somehow the grey felt yellow.

Later, the setting sun unfurled a sheet arc of light and its spokes engaged the sky into an eventual ferment. A flock of finches streamed past as the chaffinch ratcheted from the hawthorn. And then the show ended, rings of lit water expanded out over the oxbow, much as the light had done, dispersing to gone. I followed the silver trail of the coot to the stumped corner where the heron lifted and there was peace, peace curved by the course of what once was river. The subtle ripples of the water lined the reflected image of the reddened sky, and the departing heron.

Spring maintained its sedate progress and even the raucous call of the rooks seemed to have a calming beat as the day drew to a close under clearing skies. There was a March warmth radiating through the cool air, crisp with the robin's call. The babble of sound permeated the lit blossom. The day was good. The blackbird sat atop the highest birch, found the sun and looked over the hollows, where the shade of the trees created a shadow of three dimensions. I entered the meadow, and the light blown forth by the sun. I saw my shadow cast over clover and the bright structure of rookery wood before me, nests silent. The tree's linear shadows reached out a hundred yards and more; stretched. And then the rooks returned above me; bright. I felt locked to the earth. Passive and inert, yet part of the wood. A sapling reaching for sky.

I soon returned, on a day where darkness and light were shared and there was no shadow in the wood, the hollows were lit from above. The discourse of birds networked the trees like invisible branches exploring the space, and I was a node within, spoken of, to or about, I did not know, as the messages flowed through me.

Across in rookery wood, I noticed an oak that harbours a pine. Its easterly branches reaching either side of the bare trunk of the pine, the greenery above leaning away from the embrace. I stood by an alder looking out over the fields. A lone lapwing described its call in flight and the sky reminded me of a burnt out August. Lost blue and hazed, but March given away by the absence of a green darkness. Once the lapwing rested I returned. As I passed, the beech spoke of the still days when its leaves rest and the air is thick. Walking through the clover I had August on my mind, because that is what the landscape had suggested.

I continued my regular exploration of mind in spring by the oxbow. The heron rose silent from the reeds and became mist. A skylark stitched the visible air with its thread of sound. With time, the hidden sun teased the mists apart and as they lifted, trees stepped into view as the landscape was revealed. I walked the complete space of the Dove in search of returning sand martins, or perhaps it was connections I'd had before. With the sun warm, I left the river for a still pool where reflected willow created a new space, a new depth that I floated above and mind understood.

Yet it was the rooks that called me each day and from the open of the field, the hollows were bright above the shadowed meadow. Wherever I stood the brightness seemed elsewhere. The strip of rookery wood looked like a natural ribbon of black lace, a frieze against the western sky. I heard the cry of the rooks in my throat. Felt their take-off deep in my shoulders, their flight in my arms and the supporting breeze on my skin. I felt akin to all the natural forms around me. I joined the trees, and stood amongst them. Beech reached, plasticised by the light, stretched and artificial. The pines popped and cracked in the evening warmth and I existed within the sound, which fell to earth as a shadow.

Back in the hollows, concentric circles from three fowl origins ringed the sky smooth lake, like growing tree rings tracking their own time and intersecting calmly. I watched their two dimensions until my mind's eye saw three. Singing birds emitted invisible spheres of sound, expanding as ripples on water, disturbed by the trees. I imagined how beautiful they might be if time slowed and they grew, without shadow as they wrapped around everything to fill all space where there is air, fading to be refreshed and lit by the setting sun like a robin's quantum vision of gravity. I saw the blackbird cutting across the sphere of its mate's song. Stirring the sound with its beat, ripping through it and adding the whisper of its wings. A mallard cut across the circles, its sliced vee parting my vision. Returning, rooks sat in a birch, the twigs hanging down as if the bird was seeping darkness, melted by the setting sun as Venus pricked the blue above the waxing crescent moon.

Two days later, at Anslow Park, the surrounding fields were rolled to stripes and a new wind turbine was salient on the skyline. A revolving reminder of the air, its power and ubiquity, unseen like mind. The air rustled the dry oak leaves close by and hazed the far view. It danced across my skin and filled my lungs as the grass shone to white, it was as recent springs, warm and dry. The calm landscape became busy up close. A reality to my eyes that will be different to another, as all realities are subtly different and no one person, or being, can know the full landscape. To me it was joy upon joy and pleasure upon pleasure, air upon the land and I shared the reality with no one that day, just you now and your imagined reality of what was. By the pool there was a bursting calm, ridden by two coots and edged by nodding reads. Birdsong ceased, I felt alone and melted to the ground as the reflection rippled reality to a dream.

Later, I came upon a chatter of bibbed sparrows, sharing my joy, their flight about the hedgerow, the field and tree keen and buoyant; their calls were chinks of sunlight bouncing off stones, and scattered by a solar wind. I stayed with the day as it set and, denied the light, the air cooled and descended to earth to seek its warmth. So familiar am I with my chosen landscape I can be there as I please. Settled in the cooling air I was walking down the bridleway at Dunstall to meet the pooled chill at its base. To leap the hedges and circuit the trees and rise up to look down upon it all; so complete is the mental landscape. I felt overwhelming joy as this inner landscape unfurled through the boundless expanse of mind and became as one with my present reality in the air. I remained stationary and ran through the seasons, saw the leaf of the tree and snow on the branch as I travelled time and space, buoyed by the catalyst of this glorious spring day closing around me.

The next day, a pair of buzzards were about, glorying in the thermals rising from unusual spring warmth. I walked to the hollows and stood amidst the trees, turning to take them in. Each tree was art, a beauty of lit form, trunks rising beyond their ivy dressed base to curved and shadowed branches that divided to two dimensions against the blue, static as the slender pine rocked; the spiralling branches of its neighbour undulating through light and shade. Nearby, an expansive young beech had been drawn into leaf, its ridged leaves veed by the sun to the zestful green of the first canopy of spring. Birdcalls were as present as the air, the stream glistened as the clover, cutting the space with light. The hollows were calm in diffuse light and the shadows were subtle in tone. I crossed to rookery wood only to find it deserted, bar the presence of a sad silence and I felt concern for the lack of darkness. I watched black specks in the far field and two rooks arrived to circle the nests above me, their shadows rapidly climbing the trunks as they passed, but they soon departed, leaving the nests deserted.

Chapter 4

Biopsychophysis

4th April to 29th April

"The mind wanders yet deeper and farther into the dreamy mystery of the azure sky." - Richard Jefferies

At the oxbow, standing in the sudden cold and looking into the budding trees I saw a reflection of being. Before me, a swan lay on her nest with a warmth beneath I could almost feel. From my perch on the stump of the willow, I became the tree that once was. My fingered leaves felt the air as the chaffinch call explored my trunk, its accumulating call echoed by another. I felt the planet's hold as it grabbed my feet, rooting me to the ground. The air coasting through me and wrapping each organ as if each were its own. The rippling water cleansed mind as the setting sun's light broke out and tipped the arcing grass gold. This wasn't just a great place to be, I was this place and the coots ran my mirrored orange skin. The sun cast a spell on the earth and grabbed the dirt of the day from my innards. The hours of stale confined air escaped from my core to be replaced by cool light and I was returned to my host to be of nature. The sharp, cooling air sliced away the artificial grime on my skin and I was raw to the day, sensitive to its end. Embedded, the landscape was an extension of self, matter born of stars. I realised a biopsychophysis, a unity of life, mind and nature.

That night I was held firm to the ground in the silent darkness. At five, a robin lowered its rope of song and my mind climbed its strands until I was on its perch watching the sound work its way through the air, like plasma filaments extending to illuminate a willing ear. It continued to sing alone for sometime, until, in the distance, a blackbird harpooned the sky, causing others to cast forth their lines and capture the morning.

I released the new day back by the oxbow. There, I felt the solidity of the earth and depth of the space that lies upon it. As I walked, the parallax of motion described it more fully to mind, a bodily representation of the landscape that surrounds. The Dove was constant in its change, yet it remained a river. Its steady motion describing silence, as the eddies described the calls of the birds. A body of water together as my own, part of the landscape as my own. I followed its flow to the shallows where the river spoke of its bed, in whispering tones as gentle as the sun's growing warmth. The distant trees retained a solemnity of winter, their darkness fracturing the cloud beyond, the flow of the season yet to pull them into spring.

I was drawn east to the expansive flatlands of Norfolk, to be alone in the depth of the third dimension, to see the landscape unfold, walk the slate clean; to let mind spread. At Holme, the land was as flat as the sea and I felt a sense of loss. A loss of perspective, drowning in the depth of the landscape. I retreated to the wood where the depth was gauged by each tree, reducing as they stepped away and hid the distance, giving a manageable, human scale that mind could comprehend. Calibrated, I set off to the salt marsh that stuck the light, reflections capturing an essence of the landscape beyond. But more compelling were the calls, a skylark unravelling its taped eighties code, the reverse call of the lapwing, klute of the avocet and then I watched the breadth of a barn owl beneath the sounds as day came to an end.

Sculthorpe was a landscape easy to be at one with, open marsh flanked by trees, the lightening strikes of the birch, trunks shot black, clear through the rain. With the birdsong in the woods it was a heady mix, but was surpassed as four Marsh Harriers flew above the reeds. The embrace of their wings and mastery of flight in the wind and elite control was compelling. Like ash floating from a phoenix they came to rest with gentle ease, the white in their wings flashing as bright as the steady birch. Being embedded with nature, embedded with the harriers in that landscape, explains the joy such occasions can bring.

I entered deeper woods, the green flesh of bluebells, some tricked into early flower, was punctured by coppiced beech, clumped tight at the base and opening to a thicket of branches. There were aspen and birch in the wood, each its own wilderness. This thickness of flesh wasn't what I was seeking though and I returned to the coast, only to be drawn into the woods once more. The pines at Holkham that skirt the beach, but there was no green flesh here. It was the bone of barbed trunks, aggressive forms that would rip any flesh. One multi-stemmed behemoth had fallen astride the path, I veered away as it postured, enjoying the motion through the wood. The calm at its base, while the wind rifled the greenery above. Looking out to sea from the angles of the wood, the depth seemed greater, a depth beyond human existence.

Along the coast at Cley, the landscape unfolded before me again and I felt unsettled by the expanse, the mind comprehending this flatland differently. It was only through setting out and movement that the landscape was calibrated to a human scale and I realised how much of this land I could quickly cover. The wind stripped away the sounds, masking all as it ripped past. It was just self and the landscape seen, the change of air when passing from shingle to green, the sense of weight on the land, but the white noise of the wind took much away; more than silence.

The sky had a planetary scale above the salt marsh with its oozing channels; a life form in itself, dendrites carving to an axon, a tree etched into the landscape. Sea birds picked at its scalp, their feet tracking its clasping surface. Mud stained flora, matt, seaweed the only green, stretched across the mire. Black-headed gulls squabbled and cried before the beat of the mast rigging returned me to settlement.

There was a rain grey smoothness that passed to sparkles in the meadow as I noted shriek and kestrel. Rolling, billowing cloud greyed the horizon once more and I watched the light fade with thoughts in the landscape. The stripped, flat landscape, like a neutral form and base layer for all else, the essential earth that lies beneath. The flatlands extend mind and curve our thinking. As I looked up at the stars above I wondered where an extended mind might end, but if it is of no matter it cannot end, nor have boundaries. As the anthropologist and great thinker, Gregory Bateson reminds us, mind contains no things, no time, no space; just ideas of things, of time and space – news of difference from the senses. There is no inside, nor outside of mind. With our technological means, the extent of mind can reach the stars; which is both light years away and within the molecules that make us. Mind then, is everywhere; everywhere life makes sense of the world, be it a tree reaching for light or a hand reaching for bark.

Where there is nature and life, there is mind. A biopsychophysis.

※

Back in my local landscape, I stood beneath a grand willow, its trunk and branches a contorted frame supporting vertical rods patterned with fresh spring green. Drops of the previous night's rain were as intense as the sun that shone through to reflect from the brook, smooth and flat. I felt its awe first in my body, not my mind, in my chest and pit of stomach, my trunk. As I walked, the landscape seemed to circle about the setting sun, its rays as a prism beneath conquering cloud, near distant downfalls, smeared as synthetic polymers drawn below the cloud base. The trees and I cast shadows. The blackbird, beak full, was keen.

And the day changed to another in the hollows, hailstones fell down a willow bagatelle to the floor with two hops to vanish. The lake erupted as it received each nugget and the earth was sodden. As it eased the water's edge was ringed, drops from the overhanging willow completing their journey. Young maple leaves seemed to hover, level in space, in a steady cloud. Rows of young hazel leaves hung from a horizontal twig, as kippers on a tarry rod, to be seasoned by fresh air. Horse chestnut leaves hung to form a cone that pointed to the sky. There was balance in the woods.

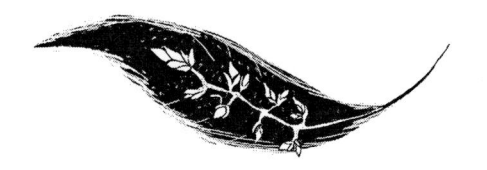

Spring's new leaves were a flashbulb recall of the year before. I felt a familiarity, a hangover from my yearlong search for deep nature and I was reminded of their depth of beauty, rather than discovering it. The weather was different than the year before, each day wet and there was a depth of mud in the hollows I'd not seen all winter. I was quietly enjoying Emerson's glory of the gloom, how the depth of grey pushes other hues forth, but I felt forsaken, if not disconnected. I stood by the swollen brook in rookery wood. Rooks gone. Brook brown. Field ploughed. Oak bare in its island of green. The lapwing returned to settle in its now ploughed base, silent. The brook progressed, constant. The chaffinch call, repeated. The sun emerged, bright. The blackbird on the hedgerow, perched. The simplicity of connection, regained. My shadow pointed, home. With the sun warming my back, the raindrops returned and I saw the crow before me shine blue. Each leaf of clover held a scattering of jewels and I waited as more fell through the joy of air to earth, my days required journey complete.

April progressed and the skylarks were as constant as the air itself at Brankley, where the ground was sodden from weeks of regular showers. I circuited towards the young birch on the ridge above me, coming into leaf once more and standing for attention, their emerging leaves fading into the greenery around. Their line became depth as I neared, until each unfurling leaf could be seen attached to bronzed and twiggy growth. Closer still, each leaf became a pair, cupped like hands, alternating to an end point and moving with the breeze. And then I was within the plantation of birch, feeling the vigour of their busy spring leaves, yet each tree still and surrounding me. A lift of spring on the sodden landscape.

Close by, the surface of the earth had been turned, revealing stones, thousands of them descending into thousands more, shrinking away. The arrival of sunlight changed the quality of the air and revealed the freshness of the larch. I'd left the constancy of the skylarks and here crows squabbled over the air, as smaller birds trilled beneath the heavy sound. At my feet, droplets ran each blade of grass. Naturally varied in spacing and sized to the width available, diminishing to a point. Each different, but each as perfect as the next, never joined, always one, magnifying the structure below. I returned my attention to the birds and I let my mind picture the three dimensions of sound layered on the landscape, which seemed to open the dense flesh of my brain into space itself. The space of the natural world is so much of our being that we exist as part of it, not divided by a lens, we fully experience its depth. And walking through the wood, along a path that reached into its heart, I saw the depth marked by blossom, fresh green of hawthorn, rowan, maple, the hanging fingers of the chestnut reaching towards the grasses and herbage below. Until I emerged to a wave of fields starred by dandelions, where a dead oak stood surrounded. Against the slate cloud it snagged the sky like inverted lightening, fallen embers about it. The depth of darkness seeped to the ground and another oak, olive green, was lit into three dimensions. It was flattened as the sun withdrew, the wind came and the cloud reached me bringing droplets of rain to soak my return.

In the fading light, once more I focussed on the joyous rotation of the landscape as I moved through it. How each pace changes the embodiment one feels as nature paints ever-changing sounds to form a multiverse of experience and pleasure in a simple series of steps. The blackbirds closing the day, the punctuation of the rook and light rain on my skin made the evening more than alive, more than alive. I watched the trees turn and I imagined each raindrop falling above me, riding the evening chorus that danced the drops through the air to their grounding.

※

At Brankley, the ground was wetter than the air and for once the wind out did the rain. Pines swayed with and then against, young birch were torn to one side, bent but keen to remain rooted in the earth, their fledgling leaves gripped by its force. A lone old oak danced its branches at the animation of it all as crows swept by. Pushing against the wind, my muscles equal and opposite to it, I felt the force of the Earth direct in the depth of my flesh. Balanced against it, I progressed, past ripped hands of chestnut, lying bright as they grasped at the bluebells. I watched the wind described by the meadow, heard it sung in a violent chorus by the trees, felt its invisible touch as it circulated the scent and taste of spring in a violent turmoil. The soaked black trunks were shot by the spring green of birch and the wood reeled and roared like some mythical beast thrashing as it sank into the depth of sea.

Back home, another world's sky pressed down on the land, plumes of volcanic ash rolling towards me, but the rooks did not bother, nested still in their bare oaks. Wetted by the day, the hollows stood in various shades of emerging green and the branches of the expansive beech hung low. Its darkened trunk spoke of the day, its leaves of spring. They detected raindrops as I stood beneath, surrounded by hidden birds, their song unimpeded by the sodden foliage. I left the wood trailing my human form as a serpent shedding its skin, to grow and renew, like the wood each spring. I could see the bones beneath my flesh, nature looking in on its self as the blackbird sat where it had before.

The River Dove brings forth and takes away, receives and gives through sound and light, is never still. I stood by the motion in the heavy rain, by the bank where twelve maple stand as one. Twelve trunks circled by hawthorn, by a curve of the river. The rain fell in dozens, the river and earth received it and I stood within it, coated and steeped in a quality of the atmosphere. It is somehow easier to realise biopsychophysis in the rain.

Chapter 5

Flesh

2nd May to 31st May

"I believe in the human being, mind and flesh; form and soul." - Richard Jefferies

May sees Earth's flesh reform. Greens ooze from the darkness of the wood, risen from the ground, as birdcalls pipe a therapeutic dose of life's spirit to its core. About the wood the meadows deepen, blades curve and take on a hint of the blue of the sky. The air itself thickens and I walk through this flesh of nature, warmed and nurtured like an organ in a greater body, pulsing with spring, beating a path speckled with blown petals from blossom. Such is the joy of May.

Within the green, the blackbird sat on its favoured perch once more, defined and as taut as its song, mapping the growing diversity as its partner spiked the lawns. In the hollows, the green started its enclosure of the paths, tightening the arteries, to slow ones progress towards the rookery. I was struck by the silence of the light. Never heard unlike water, land and air. Light is vision and carries warmth to our receptive skin, warming our flesh. Water makes sound, plays with light, captures cold and envelopes our touch; quenches and wets our flesh. Land, and that upon it, resists our touch, responds in sound and is revealed by light; that which can be consumed becomes our flesh. Air is sound, is invisible to light, has a lightness of touch and inhaled feeds our flesh.

The newly green wood, in a damp twilight had a reverential air that I almost dare not enter. Inside it was almost still, the young leaves in subtle motion, like a heat haze between us. I waited on the edge and then dived into the depth of the dark, my skin tightening as I plunged in. As my eyes adapted to the woodland light, I saw deeper, deep nature in the flesh of the Earth. And there I remained, drowning, but able to breath. For we are in nature as a fish in water.

The following day, at Corbett's Wood in the heart of Needwood, a few dozen finches, or the like, magic-ed from tree to field. Conspicuous in flight, vanished when not. Their chatter was constant, and after some time peering into the upper branches I rested my head and simply enjoyed their sound and flight, for knowing their type would have added little to the experience. Across the field, a trio of weighty branches supported a circular splash of growth, forming a compelling tree. As I crossed the field to visit it, a welcome thinning of the cloud allowed the sun's warmth through and I forgot about recent rains. The tree was an oak, busy with sound and the three branches at eight feet, became six at twelve. They meandered up through the air and its growth filled my vision and occupied my mind.

As a cell through a vein, I continued my exploration of the flesh of the local landscape a couple of days later at Drakelow Nature Reserve. The scattered song of the reed warbler bounced about the willows, like a rapid bead within a glass box. They seemed to have benefitted from a day of sunshine. Like a miss firing engine, its unpredictable notes engaged new patterns of my mind. From my spot by the reed-edged lagoon, I watched the sleeping swan wake, slowly raise its ruffled neck and seemingly yawn. After sometime slowly looking about it began to preen, as close by a reed warbler explored the density of growth; movement in the reed tops revealing its place. Rabbits fed beside me, and beyond, a coot patterned the water; a blackbird sang and I fell into its sphere of sound. The sun emerged to warm me, the swan returned to rest and I observed the stillness of a crow.

The continual rain foreshortened the landscape and the day, but extended the range of the evening birdsong. The mood of the light enveloped all and embedded mind and body in the stillness. Green upon green slid by as I flowed by the Alderbrook towards the hollows. The grey of the sky descended across the fields, yet the water still found light to shape and focus in its ripples. The light rain touched me and I felt the rings of sensation grow and fade on my skin. The feeding blackbird stood close by and I felt its presence in my flesh. Reaching the woods, drops hung on each bud of the beech, a miniature wood contained within each. As still as the air, the heron sat cloaked in its grey over the misted hollows pool. A ghost, with its reflection hanging like a bat beneath, until a passing swan disturbed it into a dream. Somehow, the air in the centre of the wood moved, as if dragged by the running water of the stream, or fanned by the gently rocking leaves, as quenched, the trees were ready to move the rain on. I stood and felt the breath of the wood on my face and when I left the air outside was still as before.

The patterns of the wind were ridden by the rooks and described by the cloud in both dimensions and colour. A palette of drama to one side of the sky, white peace to the other. Its depth of grey stained in patches by the warm hues of the unseen setting sun. It was the perfect sky to contrast the rooks and they swirled about the rookery oaks with what seemed like glee.

The next day I explored the landscape a little further. I saw the Dove floodplain as an expanse of spring green. In its centre, a crow sat still and profiled, the shadows of the trees reached out towards it as if to claim their black guardian. The river was heavy and determined, but the setting sun still able to lighten its mood with a golden stripe across the eddies and current mapped out in the surface. It tried to bring warmth to May, but the wind took it away as lone clouds patrolled the sky.

Returning to Dunstall the following day, it felt like time had taken a short cut to bring a day past to this. Time as travel, the turning of the Earth or orbit of the sun such that what was will be again. And that is how this day in May felt to me. Yet time is not circular, it is spun into patterns as our planet turns and orbits the sun as the solar system orbits the galaxy, and space itself expands. Traces like the swallows weave as they feed above the fields; the patterns of nature, the patterns of constant change. I felt that I was walking the time and space of the same landscape twice, or a parallel place, as each corner revealed a scene my mind merged to the year before. Noting what was the same within the multitude of subtle differences. The feel of the ground, the warmth of the air, but knowing there must be unseen changes in the growth of the trees. I had a fuller sense of place and what this landscape was and how it is dressed by nature each season. How one place can give the same glory each year is glory itself. And then that glory seemed captured in an orange tip butterfly resting on the burst of a dandelion. And that is the wonder of how the glory of nature can implode from the landscape and sky as a whole to the wilderness of an individual flower. For there may not be a wilderness landscape here, but there is wilderness in each tree, each leaf and flower. Learn to see that wilderness and pleasure is all around. Then I realised the wettest drought I'd known had discouraged my previous years regular evening trips here and I was missing the place, or maybe we were missing each other, such was the connection: we exist of nature's mind.

※※

Each wood, and each tree within, was a bright mass of May green; especially the beech at

Brankley. Their greens lifted the inner wood and left it open for vision to explore. The wind carried air explored it too. And the light. I found a recently uprooted pine, the dry circle of lifted soil about its roots was almost white. In the pit beneath, pebbles, shaped by water, were exposed to light once again. The fine roots hung down, forlorn, reaching for earth. Nearby, rooted grasses were keenly upright, too low to be dragged by the wind like the throngs of supple beech leaves they pointed to above. I stood by a footpath, an imprint of years of human passage; the subtle whites of the cow parsley were drifting in to deepen its inscription on the land. A lone swallow worked the air, an orange tip butterfly flew the path to the first parsley bloom, as zephyrs brushed the meadow grass and I went deeper into the flesh of the landscape, tunnelled by the wood; consumed. When I emerged, my thoughts were with the nightingale, its place and late song of May. Where is that bird that entwined my heart last solstice?

As men on wheels rode the landscape, and a lone woman ran, I sat within it. There were curious lambs in the fields, fresh trees surrounding and jackdaws about them. I watched how the flight of a crow played with the light, which then revelled with the swallows. Silent, I heard jaws at work behind me and turned slowly to see what seemed like the nose of a serpent. Obscured by the grasses, but visible and moving nonetheless.

The simple contours of the landscape spoke to me as they rolled away. A constant, yet ever fresh message saying what needed to be heard. Each tree a new voice, each bird a song. I walked towards a pair of old oak, and looking back didn't want to leave until I'd understood their form. One was a spring green, its classic oak form angled left. The other was a shade more yellow, with a higher reaching trunk, clear within its middle. They were both in constant motion within their shape, and as I watched, the sky cleared and the light described their dimensions more fully. I eventually left through younger trees and felt the life within the smooth, stout ash and the lithe dancing of the birch; its young leaves green, tipped crimson, like berries from afar.

The following day the sun was still struggling to get a hold on May and the head of a yellowhammer was the most intense brightness. The banks of the oxbow were white and yellow and the cygnets hid amongst the reeds. I carried on to where the river spoke. A willow had collapsed into the Dove and I paused by it. On the bank of the flood defence, a drift of buttercups fell away to spill out and flood the meadow with yellow. Daises sat tight waiting for warmth. When I returned the six cygnets were in open water, their necks the same silver as the clouds and I felt the joy of new life. Close by were two young coots with shaggy blazoned heads, a parent's explosive pitch sending them back to the nest.

True May warmth and light finally arrived and I felt compelled to remind myself of evenings in the late spring. The breadth of the lit blades of grass in the woods and illuminated seed heads across the fields. How the stillness carries evening song. How the vapours mist the fields and form a dew. How the cool air pockets within the land. How the light enriches tone. How figures are lost into the darkness of the trees. How the landscape becomes immersive. How we are flesh of flesh.

The sun, an ignited harvest moon, rounded on the wooded horizon to close the year's warmest day. I let its faded light mark my retina and watched that image once the sun had fallen from view. When the sun falls, woods are at their most animalistic and I felt their breath; a firm breeze that only seemed to exist within, as the massed trees exhaled the warmth of the day through a complex diversity of forms.

The change of state continued as unusual cold turned to unusual warmth. At Brankley, a forever sun cast a shadow of the lone oak to the meadow. I stood at its edge, looking at this reduced form of oak, how it lay upon the grasses. How this two-dimensional form quivered with the breeze and the canvas was in motion too. Then I thought of the three dimensions in this shadow, I saw only where it fell, yet there was an image of oak all the way from tree to ground and I stood within it, became the canvas too. Felt the coolness of this oaks shade and the change in light. Behind me, my own shadow merged with that of the oak on the meadow so that as the tree blew my form became apparent only to then disappear from this patch of landscape. I moved on to where my shadow could encompass a young birch and our forms merged.

The wood about the leaning oak was a magic of light and natural forms. Passing bluebells and keenly emerging ferns, upright, individual, reaching for the sun. There was a heartbeat of birdsong and the lit foliage and shadow danced about space. The green of the pasture beyond was silvered and blue, with wind drawn seed-heads and nodding bluebells spent. There were drifts of yellow and explosions of hawthorn throughout the wider valley, but with unfixed gaze it was greenness and sky blue. I sat and exchanged reflected light with a distant oak and saw calmness in its form, but it was more than its shape, I was compelled by its active, steady poise and standing on the land. To my eyes it felt as part of me as my flesh, or my flesh felt part of it. At its base, the breeze described a river along the grasses of the valley floor, constant with tidal surges that broke across unseen banks. The green waters rode invisible rocks that moved their place and disturbance of the flow; and then I saw time-lapse clouds drifting across the green.

Such was the new found warmth, I waited for the day's close heat to unfold to a quiet breeze before walking deep nature again. Such is the demise of the cuckoo I hoped the one that called wasn't as alone as the setting sun. It likes the flatlands of the Dove where its call can travel the void left by lost brethren; for now its joyful repeat has become a reminder of decline. And I felt sorrow for the nightingale too, which I tried to hear in every song of another until the half-moon lit the sky, for a May evening without them is darkness. A darkness as deep as the blackbird that closed the day.

    I channelled the paths at midnight, through scented night air that livened dull senses. Adapted, I saw trees flat against the half-moon light, unseen pigeons breaking cover and rising into the settling coolness. Tired from night excursions I came to rest beneath a birch in the sunshine the next day; my eyelids lit red as drops beat the leaves. Risen, I caught the days end at the oxbow. A black carp only two thirds submerged circled in the shallows; calmly powered by its caudal fin, coot black and crow size, long dorsal limp to one side. Deep greens were taking control of the landscape as I pushed on through leaves large, spiked and water bound. A kingfisher banked by and the dark clouds rolled and trailed, drawing a landscape of hills. A flood of cupped yellows blazed the flat meadow, such that curlew and peewit of Yorkshie Dales were in my mind. At rest with the motion of the shallows, I felt the weight of the oak on the unfurled plain. A blackbird arrested the evening fall from the bough of an ash and I wanted the weight of a mountain.

    May came to its close and I was shouldered by the green vigour of the hollows, its breath static, each leaf suspended, all held, all still. Each bloom able to be received from any angle. All held. All still. I left to a Saturn sky of grey and yellow, ringed by the green depth of trees, moon gibbous, clouds lit lunar bright. I sat caged by the evening song, under cuckoo and clearing skies until the silence of the night air. Then it struck me, that the air is the breath of the flesh of the Earth.

Chapter 6

Lived Mountains

1st June to 18th July

"Over the open hills, up the steep ascents, mile after mile, there was deep enjoyment in the long-drawn breath." - Richard Jefferies

June came with a new landscape. With a call as coarse as rock, jackdaws squabbled on the mountain side as a blackbird remained still, a voice of calm pouring over the confusion as I sat high above Coniston Water; within the gravity of the hills. I could almost sense the land falling away to the valley and rising up afar, like a synaesthesia of sight and mass. The jackdaws' calls were like stones within a gorge and I soon tuned to the subtle eddies of sound fluid in-between. They were as smooth as flowing liquid, flavouring the air, and I let the sounds be colours, like ribbons through the sky, until my perch became an altitude of flight. I soared down to taste the mass of water. I was met by a pied wagtail in its skeletal suit, and there time seemed to pool, to a pause in the lake, its surface a reflection of the landscape in a matt foil that made the trees columns of green in this temple landscape. Time pooled, the landscape still.

The next day I visited the Old Man of Coniston, but not without destination, I needed to get to the top in order to free the mind from the summit. As I walked I tried to understand the timescale of this mountain's living. The trees like gnats on flesh to this geological being, each tree a blink of an eye to the mountain. The lichens the only life that can begin to understand the mountain's time. Mosses devoured boulders and trees, as brown leaves waited to return to earth. Ash and fern were bright against the black brook. I skirted the base of the mountain and felt the firm resistance that felt somehow hollow beneath. I walked up to beyond where trees can grip its side, but the skylark still sang, describing the falling crags and scree; the rock defined under bright skies by abrupt shadow. I, like many others, pitted myself against the slopes to the summit, a place to take in the landscape, not defeat it. It was good to push against the slope and feel the force of the mountain's gradient. The air was crisp with height and the Old Man touched with icy fingers like frozen glass. From the summit I saw people cradled in the landscape. We gather where nature is most kind; below the hills, on the level where there's water and shelter from prevailing winds. Here, landscape, nature, time and human meet to form place.

I listened to how the Old Man speaks, in many simple tongues when the conditions are so mild. Each stream a whisper and the fledgling becks surrounded me. Each step revealed a different voice describing different points of the fragmenting mountain. Amongst the space between, a bird hammered the fells with its call. As I sank into the valley, I held the rising moon constant on the ridge. Where the trees tube the beck, mosses climb the trunks as the plants gather around the mountain's outflow, drinking it in, concealing it from view such that the light becomes other, almost trapped, and the water roars in protest as it falls to the flatness of that massed below. A birch, each of its three stems as stout as a trunk, bouldered out across the water; branches welded to one another as rust welds finds from the sea floor. Rowan, with the occasional larch and oak, formed their own green spate above the water. A green flow billowing out of the gorge and splashing into the sky; a spray of ferns lying further up the mountain side.

Downstream, I passed an ancient quarry, a cliff-face of falling ivy by the river, its entrance caged by a many-branched oak. Its trunk horizontal, roots clenching an outcrop like torrents of water about a boulder, poised like a nimble beast on a wall. In the calmer waters, the reflected gorge was a mystical land, where the air is green vapour and the trees translucent to light. Diving in would see one raise up from the earth to be translucent too, taking on the green, unable to grasp the trees, but able to pass through them.

Ice grey skies drew the heat from the day and smoke from open fires scented the cold air. My eyes were drawn to the blackness rather than silver in the lake and even the birdsong had an icy air. With a noise like a rapid ping-pong with glass, two dozen jackdaws gathered about a chimney, smoked to the colour of their snood, by the burning black coal below. They worked the sound into a frenzy whilst a hierarchy was established on the perches. Those at the base were always looking up and there was a few seconds of silence, before positions were rejected and the jostling started again. Yet, there was calm, as the smoke of carbon described the motion of the wind as it rose to disappear. As the light faded, the greens were transformed to those of the darkness of midsummer, the air was a slow chill, floating a sheet of cloud over the fells.

The next day I took to water and floated within the landscape, drifting with the wind and feeling the subtle waves as the hills sat within cloud. With the stillness of air, the clouds hung still below the ridge opposite and even the smoke from the chimneys didn't want to rise, remaining still, gathering into the greyness to be pierced by the birds singing the end of the evening rain. Eventually, the cloud lowered further and took the landscape, leaving just a single stroke of hill and a few fields with oak, still standing above their shadow, even in the scant light.

The next morning the fells were sliced by cloud, with jackdaws providing the sound of the fracturing hills. A blackbird and thrush paused from feeding to perch, as a couple of dunnock walked a wire, wings fluttering. I walked to Guards Wood in a light, invasive rain. The hillside of Yewdale Crag was split by the tumbling waters of White Gill. Cloud clung to the heights like the trees as I walked along Yewdale Beck to Tarn Hows wood, with its coppiced hazel, oak, rowan and rugged young birch twisting an existence. Birch reflect their landscape and environment, from black barked with runt leaves to the long and slender. And here, the copper trunked, piping the goodness to a spray of leaves. Nearby, a mossed oak screamed orange, a fallen branch leaving a six foot scar. I trod clasping roots and glistening rock, beside mounds of common haircap moss, starred like a deep field view of the universe. A cloud blew through the wood, a nebula of vapours to feed the mosses. Out of the wood, swallows traced the curved fields in the sweeping landscape above Coniston Water, a simple compelling circuit that returned me to the lake. There, a black-headed gull was powered by its force field reflection, against the dark reflected mass of the trees. A crow's other was not apparent, seemingly powered by darker forces, the unseen matter that pervades. From the shore, I looked out on time: the eons of the hills, centuries of oak, decades of birch and years of young rowan. The days of fledgling dunnock and seconds of the raindrop, falling to make its way into the bedrock and aquifers before becoming level in the lake.

❋

Back home from the fells, after a day of down pouring, the river touched its bank tops and in places explored beyond. Its bed deeply submerged, it spoke of its banks in a turmoil of currents; at capacity to evacuate the hills. The sound of river through willow and ash, flows embracing trunks and branches, masking the dragging of the leaves. Taught flows within a mass, as the dark blades of swifts cut the currents in the air above.

June had been taken by a cool greyness that even the swifts could not sculpt to joy. Although spring had been cool, the green darkness of the trees seemed early, the long days failing to ignite. The environment gave little and shaped thought to a clay. The blackbird had little evening brightness to imbibe and release to spark the morning and there seemed to be a danger of a spiral of decline. Beyond the hollows, there were no swallows, no patterns above the crop-lined fields that map the subtle contours of the land. I wanted to cast off the clothes of this failing season unable to find the joy within it. Until, at Dunstall, where baubles of redpoll had decorated the birch, I heard a tree pipit.

Its song seemingly based on eons of observation as it described the fall of a leaf to the ground. As I left, neon pink and orange dog rose plastered my sight. Traversing the hillside, I felt the Earth pulling me towards its core as a leaf leaves its tree. My mind explored the crust, flowed down with magma, hidden yet known.

As wet days flowed into one another I fully realised the fascination of rain at the interface. Rain is bright at the interface. Rain sounds at the interface. Rain clings to the interface. Rain becomes lens at the interface. Its energy dissipates at the interface. Whether it is hard human abstractions, or other nature. Rain at the interface is how rain is best heard, seen and considered. Where its existence is most apparent. Where rain becomes wet. Where rain gathers. Where rain ends. Where rain and flesh share a moment of being one. But the rain did not end, and another wet day arrived with Brankley a purple meadow. Earth decorated my calves and shins, as yellow and white blooms decorated the purple field. The mauve grasses dressed the land in a soft matt haze as a shard of cinnabar moth crossed the purple dream and the oak stood hard within. Such is their missing, and my yearning, I saw blown summer leaves as swallows carving patterns in the air about the trees. The cool greyness was dissonant to the season and it argued with the fauna. Along the deep green of a path less trodden, a light blue egg lay before me, and I wished it could hatch the clear blue skies of summer.

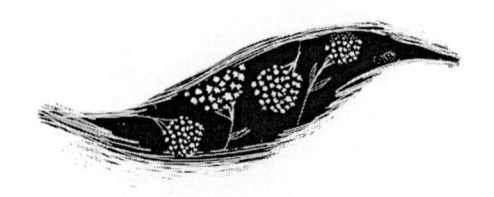

And overnight it did. In the hollows, the dense green was shot by elderflowers, an impact of white spread on an impenetrable green. A snipers vain attempt to retreat the green that engulfs the wood and tries to hide the sky. Within, the lung of wood was dense with green, pulsing with sound, as ash gasped at the breadth of day shown within the sky; the first sky of scale of the season. I looked up to see a sword fight of swifts, their solid wings flashing in the early sun like eight blades. It was the first day of summer at midsummer's solstice and the air was as fresh as polished steel. Greenfinches scribed the metal with their call of lazy summer's days and the inadequacies of the summer so far were forgotten. Under a closing sky of June, a blackbird told of its day and year, for soon it shall sing no more. The sky moved slowly, trying to halt time so the blackbird's song should never end. Part of the sky darkened and took the birds form, but it had no voice and returned to drifting cloud. I felt that the sky, and evening itself, was a feather against a globe. And that globe was an eye within a bird, a blackbird with a body lost in the blackness of space. It was solstice and the day was balanced like equinox.

At Anslow Park, I stood by the pool until the sun shone. Watching the wind blown ripples make it a river and reflections pair it green. I saw granite in the heron and granite take flight. I felt the g-forces of the sand martins as they flew, their patterns as fascinating as the stillness of the hovering kestrel. I stood for so long that when my daughter took my hand, I felt the hand of nature. Touched by the landscape, and that which is part of it, the sun withdrew and I saw tears of joy on the wild rose.

June produced a summer's evening and I was taken by the ash before a wind sculpted cloud. Its billowing nature almost still, but standing I heard its gentle breath as shrill swifts diced. In the village, flags hung limp and the brook was a slow conveyer of fallen leaves. Glutinous air carried scents of nature, refined oils burnt and a blackbird to land on green. Ordered thatch transformed reeds to sharp human lines, above red clay baked into blocks and around trunks squared and sawn to lengths.

It had been the wettest April through June on record and the landscape at Brankley was sodden, with standing water over paths. Yet the grasses, rockets and their trails, launched from the field margins that were full of purple, yellow and white. The foliage deposited water on me and that from the trees beat the ground. A grounded red admiral butterfly beat its wings slowly in a mechanistic manner, as if wound, before reaching a temperature for lift off; June's brightness still intense. I felt a desire to mould wet earth and create new forms from sodden clay, to bake in the sun's warmth; but what could I create that satisfied more than nature's forms? The water stained beech eyed me and spoke through gaping gash. I felt a sodden plight, an aqua inebriation.

July by the Dove and rain still fell, like wind blown reeds, in drifts that sounded the wetness. A grey intensity in form and sound that cloaked the landscape so that it stepped away into the gloom. But the swifts did not stall as they stole the sound of a passing express, trees nearby blown to show their silvered undersides grey. Not content with wetting the land, the iron grey cloud flung down misshapen eruptions of yellow stained vapours, as if to grasp the Earth. I sought refuge in the woods, finding a pool of darkness, reflected trunks sinking into a deep pit with shafts of light. The blackbird shared the woodland darkness and its alarm call stitched across the gloom like a beak orange thread. The floodwaters claimed the land either side of the raised path and I continued along a suspended walkway between two bright canopies. Birds caressed the woods with flight more gentle then their song, lifting threads from branch to branch and across more open glades. My neurones mirrored their route and chemistry ensued, revealing these words and inducing contented calm. Until I was farmed by flies, extracting my blood and feeding my mind with thoughts to move on. I found wetland pools that weighed the land like dead weight on tarpaulin, water spiked by grasses covering stony earth, fading to a depth of brown that reflected the cloud baring sky set to replenish. Over the meadow, the water spread and grasses hung like green rain from the mirror clouds.

The gathered clouds held the landscape still. The greens drank in the grey and the landscape of my journey sat, ill defined like folds in tissue on the horizon to the north. The poise of trees in still sodden air against dark toned skies had become the state of summer. It allowed the birdsong centre stage and the trees themselves to be examined in constant form.

Silt from risen water lay crazed on the banks of the Alderbrook, and sodden, deep sludge slipped the slope to the ford; tracked and imprinted, such that if baked and left for millennia it might be found as fossil traces of human progress. Elsewhere, carried logs and beaten greens dragged the bank, as fine rain hung about to dusk the evening prematurely. A line of dark shower clouds trailed the landscape, slug like, with glistening back, trailing the land as it made steady progress. Birdsong pitted by the beat of light rain found space in the saturated air. Silted paths, surface rain beaten to pewter, were patterned with leaves in sodden decoupage; as sprigs of ash against the leaden sky.

July was May in feel, but in the hollows, golden chestnut leaves were blighted to fall. Those still engaged with the young host were wilted and yellowing above; a rasping crow captured the despair. The shining black serpent of the wood, which lay under the narrow stream, was silted to brown. There was a faint trace of the floods, stained leaves and flattened grasses swept the banks; evidence of the temporary, yet dramatic immersion. A few swallows tried to sketch new trees by the old rookery wood, but there were too few to sculpt form. Instead, the quick five worked linear patterns along the edge of the trees. At times wings clasped to body, bulleted, before working the air again to rise. Then dropping and turning with wings outstretched, above lank clover and mired earth, as a closing white sun blackened the hill crested trees.

I continued to walk the pathways, always having destination, yet giving freedom to explore. I arrived where waters met. Eddies spiralled as envisioned minds might, teased from their host walking through the landscape. In the flatness of the oxbow, three crows perched in a hawthorn, like wind drawn shreds of black plastic caught in the thorns. A blackbird sang from within, its final song of summer? Muffled by wind and willow, it reeled me back to see a mistle thrush. An extinguished dying sun hung in the wet gloom like a lone ember in ashes, drowning in the promised end of summer's rain. The splashes from its exit ran down my fingers, cool and clung to their tips. As I stood within the rain, I was reminded how much landscape is tied to weather. And if our being extends into the landscape, then our being extends into the clouds; perhaps that is why we feel the mists so. From the rains of Coniston, to those of the Dove, I'd realised that the viewed landscape is mind and being human is being in the landscape, whether it is the lived flatlands or lived mountain.

Chapter 7

Fragments of Summer

22nd July to 26th August

"Nature has affixed no bounds to thought." - Richard Jefferies

After three weeks of July I was able to walk the familiar landscape by the Dove in more familiar summer weather. Sun as constant as the river, hovered by dragonflies amidst the buzz of others. Their whirring, machined and mechanical flight described wires as a yellowhammer passed. I let the alder be the centre of my gaze and movement in order to garner as much as possible about its reality. The sky extended longer than the land, curving and capping the landscape. Finally, the sky was blue, a flat depth above, always a backdrop however high the swifts fly. I heard the river over the wind at the shallows and felt a more immediate connection to mind, a wormhole through blown interference. I stood in the heat as five chasing swifts became twelve, rising until they scraped the sky, their blades slicing its limits, fragments of sound falling like sparks from punctures that would become stars.

Swifts extend the mind in a special way, their flight teasing and carding it so that it is disentangled from the everyday, to network the mind with sky. Their journey and remarkable flight, seemingly rigid and dark forms, like scythes on rails cutting the air, twisting, constantly adjusting their bodies about flexing articulations, as heads remain static. Shallow unconscious eyes always parallel to the ground, feeding nonreflective minds. Anodised blades cutting thoughts free to float with them in azure skies.

The evening calmed to an oblique blue and time had stolen July. I listened to the blackbird's final boast of summer, its song a twine for thoughts to climb and board a vessel of reflection, riding an ocean of greens, canopy hues that splash the air of sky and deny it'll ever be autumn. Aboard and skyward, my sail was weaved by a weft swift, through warp jute threads on the sky loom. Each note of the song a stich, every flourish a tie so to capture the breath of summer to journey to a place where trees puddled the fine dusk horizon, pools of blackness against a trace of setting sun.

August, and the young chestnut in the hollows stood shed, bare as all about were green. Birds were silent and the wood was at the zenith of its breath. Paused, air hung still in the pit of the lung and the bell of St Mary's tolled long and repeated until a line call of dusk answered. As the blackbird's wings blurred, its core shrank away to be lost in the darkness called night, its wake a veil of dark silence across the freshness of the trees as the season fell into a still and tired calm. Out in the open the clouds mapped out a new globe and it was time to travel to the landscapes of Northumberland.

There, at Bamburgh, the patterned beach was mirrored in the clouds and the breeze was a breath I felt I could exhale; long, a rushing of mind into the landscape, the power of this place is such that I must return. My shadow reached for an edge of mind, but on the beach here at sunset there is no angle oblique enough to reach where the landscape takes one's thinking. The sunlight bounced the sand, a skimming pebble on flat calm waters. The constant sea was mind as it played my brain, bringing it about through interaction.

Coast changes mind as a wave washes the rocks. And sea is like mind, deep and unknown, with the waves our purposeful consciousness. Where black rocks slope down to sea I found the place right for me, at that time and moment it was where the landscape made the right mind. The fractured and irregular, lichened and barnacled host was both of sea and of land. The sea was life itself, surveying the landscape, settling in lowlands and briefly asserting summits. Where it stayed long enough, plants and shell-life gripped, changing the landscape, bringing others. Here the swallows did not map trees, they piloted ravines and sketched the crags beneath, a reminder of how landscape changes mind. I moved on, to the expanse of Budle Bay, without pathways until the pools of water forced me onto the raised landscape. Rooks and jackdaws scattered the mown meadow with calls and a butterfly passed as a flown harebell. Under uniform light and silver grey sky, terns flew as swallows of the sea. I looked out and saw common scoter, four gannet and a resting of eider ducks, and then set off back. Returning, the pale expansive sands were sea, all footprints gone. Part of the wonder of the beach is that each new day is without pathways. Like newly fallen snow, the revealed beach is a landscape cleared of human habit, like the habit that steers our thought. It is a place for exploratory thinking, which can only find new paths as new paths appear; fired by some random component, which when away from the renewal of the tide can evolve into more permanent ideas. And just as each pathway laid down on the beach cannot be separated from the footsteps that created it, mind cannot be separated from being; both are formed from our presence in the landscape.

From the dune above Bamburgh much can be seen. The sea and its version of the sky, from greys through silver, to blue and smudges of darkness where the showers lie, transforming Lindisfarne from sunlit detail, to monochrome. To the east, tracks through corn revealed the contours of the landscape. Bamburgh Castle doesn't so much rise from the dolerite outcrop, but the rock and foliage creeps up its sides to consume its straight lines, leaving the curved turrets until that first conquest is complete. From my perch, I wondered why the landscape of Northumberland seems more extensive. The wider sky with higher clouds stretching out the land to a more distant horizon. Summits, however small pose these questions and give context. The eyes and brain itself does not see, but enable the mind to access and be the wider landscape. They broaden the mind, as the flatlands. And of course, summits provide a significant place in our interpretation of landscape, from which to observe. And from this, the most modest of summits, I returned from reflection to viewing and saw an acknowledgement and settling of jackdaws, a chase of swallows, an arrival of rooks, passing of crows, an arching of grasses and the shadows of drifting clouds; patterns on patterns of sea and land. I felt the touch of breeze and heard the constant chirp of sparrows, like numerous points of light upon the sea. All from the summit of a simple dune.

I returned to the beach, to calm silver pools and the pulse of breathing waves. The sea breathed upon the rocks, pointed blue on blocks of grey through black of shadow, with oystercatchers there too. I walked the wet sand that resists like bone, then gives like flesh.

I changed my mind by changing place, to the East Neuk of Fife, and the thick sea mist was certainly cause for change. It brought mint freshness to the air, just as vision was dulled. And I realised how mist is connective, it restricts vision and bounds the mind to the immediate landscape. When Crail was unveiled from the sea mist, it was as still as the day before, and looking out, the horizon was lost in a far mist that joined sea and sky. The rocks of West Ness reached out to touch the mystery as a shanty rose from the harbour, as the lifeboat came in. With time, the landscape returned to the fore and the tide brought the sea to the reaching rocks, where crows became lost amongst the many shadows. With clouds patterning the sea from shore to horizon, I watched constant waves covering and revealing a heart of rock, a pulse of nature to synchronise with our own. Plants grasped the walls built against the water and as the light faded the horizon became a disc around the Earth, like a ring of Saturn, bright and thought blue.

The next day, the Isle of May was revealed, a faded silhouette, a tailless, chimneyed whale and I thought of place surrounded by sea, where mind must be different again. Here, at my place on the mainland, the exit of the swifts and swallows will deny the mind of the thoughts that can occupy free space; quick, creative slices of inspiration or soaring visions, difficult to discern and capture as they sweep and glance the edges of mind. And as the clarity of the air improved further, the Isle of May became a landscape with features, shear cliffs with vertical lines of shadow and rolling green that ebbed away to be level with the sea. It added form, but the further detail of life could only be imagined and placed there; life on May could not extend to here in August.

Walking along the coast I found a small bay with geometric patterns in the sand. Humans brushing a hexagon of large circles, each sharing a smaller hexagon of its own, such that there were thirty-six circles around the one at its centre. Each of the main seven had a further twenty-four small satellites, clustered in diamonds, between its six shared moons to make a pattern of 181 circles of three sizes on the beach. When complete the creators viewed their work from the cliff top, temporary in the landscape, unrecognised by those arriving on the beach, who trailed across and scraped its regularity away before it was lost to the tide. One product of shared minds on the beach, feeding other minds and tracing them still now.

By morning, there was cloud, but enough brightness to line the horizon west, while east Bass Rock was underlined by the darkest grey and the Isle of May was a whale once more. Up the coast at Tentsmuir, seals wailed as wind around wires. Ghosts of eider circuited and distant gulls scattered like the shells close to my feet. Later, I sat where the rocks nose like turtles, until I was forced on by the tide. Pigeons returned to the harbour, riding with their partner like a shadow, gulls circled, catching the evening sun; how it must glint in their eye and capture their minds as they cry. They perched where the sun still fell, parent and child, lone and calling. Swallows and swifts tied the scene and gave distance to the sea bound cloud which reached for the pink hued Bass Rock, cave like with its shadow; Berwick Law, a pulse in the landscape, to the east.

By nightfall, the view became a ribbon of lights where others are experiencing and sharing mind; a string of ideas on a clean slate. I was looking for a landscape that can be read and the skills and knowledge to read it. Long ago we read and spoke the landscape, then wrote it down so it could be learnt, forgetting in the process how the landscape itself is read. Landscape is part of mind, not an abstraction, which is why a view is never fully taken home. One last look will never be enough to keep it in mind, as the landscape itself is part of mind; part of the mind of place.

Back home, the August silence of the birds crossed my contemplation. Woodpigeons clapped, paths were webbed and then there was the silence of bright green; its flesh damp with dew, the leaves as bright, crossed by dark shaded trunks. The August wood contrasts the summer light and the birds were as silent and hidden as mammals. A sparrowhawk, straight tail trailing, drifted and a mute blackbird dreamt by, as silent as the clouds painting the blue, as quiet as light falling on the birch leaves, that shone, lit and shadowed. It all spiralled my contemplation to galaxy proportions as vaporous clouds teased lines and butterflies crossed like birch leaves released. A burst sphere of dandelion seed rode unseen air, and higher, another, with its own direction. A magpie paddled the precious light, until pistons pumped their roar, foot down human pedalling ices and tunes filled the quiet air.

The cloud was low, hanging well below the blue and glowing like it was birthing a small sun, shafts of light pointing to its location, from where it might fall. Beyond, people suspended by hot air set themselves above the bright horizon. And reaching Brook Hollows I found where the light had fallen, deep in the lake, which became a sky blurred with a path of light flown by a lone swallow; then me into the wood. Its light was subdued, dimensions apparent, it surrounded me and thus became mind, thought and time. A silver thread of birdsong reeled me through and the heron was ancient, a form of other time rising through the now to a place bursting with such space that it too could have landed the new sun.

The host cloud, now unburdened, shrank away to mask the enclosed hot air and east it was a different day, a different experience, a different mind. The copper beech gaped and the mapped habit trodden in the earth dissected flesh, to become wound that only our absence can heal. Amidst and within plantation rows, mind became more human once more, the sky spoke of little and the landscape read like lined paper before the story was written. Yet beneath the page, I could sense a story buried within the earth, of all that has been and passed this place across time. It was that which moved me on to tread and read the landscape further. It was then that the setting sun cast a single six foot wide beam across the clover to reveal the dust of insects in a space free of swallows and martins. As its hue deepened, the sun continued to explore the landscape from new angles and through new spaces, until I reached ground high enough for its beam to bridge the lower ground and I became its opposite pier, until it sank and I was left feeling the stillness of the atoms in the air.

Its blades beating the grasses, a dragonfly 'coptered, circled and span away, its course mirroring the oxbow that enclosed a field of coming autumn hues, punctuated by pigeons that lifted to score and beat the sky. It was still enough to feel the hidden sun and hear the sounds travelling the flatlands. The painter's alder, frozen in its exploration of space, offered itself from every angle, each degree, minute and second. Branches preferring air and water had contorted the solid to its leant form, and in opposition they balanced until I saw the tree for the first time as two parts; that of air and that of water, the latter falling away. Then a spectacle of sand martins rode the air as a stream rides boulders, before returning direct, as the weeds rode the current of the shallows below. As I sat, a constant repeated call could be heard, the slow dripping away of summer continued.

Days later at Blithfield, as August drew towards a close, a canopy bird picked at mind and smaller cousins echoed the height of the wood, expanding the unseen. Looking out through a clearing, the bright landscape shone as ferns and briers brushed by. Standing, time slowed, there was no breeze to stretch or mark the transient and it was only my movement that created time. The stagnant pond was a pierced sheet of green, plastic, artificial and skimmed. As I walked, stepping-stones of light always escaped my descending foot and time kick started as the wood became dynamic; breeze motioned leaves and tumbling squirrels. Felled trees lay, new pathways of mind, creating thoughts. Where trees still stood, the air cooled and mind was calm.

Plants over-reached their space and time and were set to tumble. Within the reeds, warblers grumbled rather than sang and from time to time perched, revealing mechanical movements from within their tiny frame. Squared batons angled down the loosestrife to where they twist and split when dry. Purple blooms, topping their height, were delved by bees in search of summer's sweetness. A tumble of young birch had a freshness of spring and the sharp leaves of the willow cut the light to reveal its brightness. A snag tree stood amongst the green, a symbol of remembrance to come as summer leaves. I stood in the cool of the birch, its hanging branches framing the late August lagoon; clouds of trees were repeated and drawn below, stretching across the calm to the water touched by the breeze, such that points of light seemed to flow as a galaxy expanding. Where the young birch had turned and purple loosestrife spiked the herbage, there was an impressionist vision of late summer. Fragments of summer were beginning to litter the ground as its form weakened and the outer shell started to shed. Summer was shedding its skin and golden fragments flew and lay below; a collapsing star, an unsustainable final bloom.

Chapter 8

Being

1st September to 22nd October

"A fresh footpath, a fresh flower, a fresh delight. The reeds, the grasses, the rushes—unknown and new things at every step—something always to find; no barren spot anywhere, or sameness." – Richard Jefferies

Movement in flight describes a different being, a different mind. The steady lines of the dragonflies, hovers and spirals of the kestrel and easy glides of the buzzard all describe being in their own way. Just as the sounds of the grasshoppers and calls of the birds do: those that sing, the tuneful and tuneless, short phrases and long, repetition or variation; screeches, squawks, hoots and coos. The discourse of birds, echoing and giving depth to the complex and intense wider mind of the wood, extended by the matrix of song and network of trees. The open mind of space, where thinking can float as the clouds; their arrangement in the sky, with the position of the sun and place of the Earth itself, which brings leaves to the trees and forces their surrender. At each place, at each hour of each day, there are many thousands of stories, all add and change mind.

September was calm, warm and reflective. A fish leapt and returned with the sound of a pearl dropped into water: glossy, spherical; a globe of sound. The stillness of the oxbow was a canvas for the chattering of birds, and the silence of the blackbird. The river flowed like light itself, individual brightness's further diffused by the leaves of a hanging willow. The flow of water and lazy flight of the heron. Hosted thistledown spread across the plain in stillness and bright suspense, untroubled by the teasing air, patient in a contentment of place as I watched the heron's silence.

A few days later at Brankley, a September shine of ash and larch hid the decay below, spires of browned foxglove vertical in the light of the forest floor, a rain of breeze and hinging of laden branches filled the air. Trees to the fore were lucid and dimensioned, those afar hazed by a blue vapour of constant September sun. Only the birch could feel the breeze and it was a landscape in calm, with occasional breaks of birdsong preventing a fall to dream. Had it been May, the skylark would have narrated the day, but it was a scene best described by the call of the crows. In the wood, shafts of sunlight printed the leaf litter like water lilies on a pool. Here, a sweet chestnut, beech, birch and pine formed a square that was somehow a circle. I stood the soft earth at its centre, beneath the green leaves projected and arrived in the landscape. As the sun descended, the heat withdrew and the crow was at its blackest, crisp silhouette against the exhausted sky. Hips rose in vibrance as the last light's colour complimented their hue and the west was a golden hill, bright of cheviot form, rolling the horizon beneath a direction of geese and more solid black corvids against the elemental afterglow. The lucidity of the trees fled west as I left the landscape and the dream lifted to the sky where it spread so that it spanned consciousness itself. When sky becomes mind, earth becomes body.

Back at Brook Hollows, on another day of being, a robin was a point of calm within the stillness. As light is focused by a lens, the robin was present on a perch, like a projection of the landscape, and I was in its horizon of calm. Dozens of martins, stomachs golden from the African sun, scattered about rookery wood. Feeding in a pattern, that stretched would span a continent. And then they rose and departed, and I felt summer disappear with them; I sensed the leaves shrivel and die as golden clouds fell to consume and stain the trees, while I was stranded in beaded clover.

By mid-September at Dunstall, briers, pumped red with the vitality of a season's growth, hung the hedgerows, that in places were shrouded by the spent herbage of summer. In the sun, the ash still spoke of spring, the oak of midsummer and grasshoppers of some place, not time. The cherry was leading the season, turning its hue and releasing the past. And I walked through these time zones and places on just one short pathway. The one in a hundred years wetness of summer was leaving the earth and it was dry underfoot, leaving the eyes free to take the mind into the canopy. Pathways allow more than just easier travel between places; the trouble free ground frees the eyes and allows effortless attention to the landscape and nature surrounding. Our rivers of human habit allow the mind to extend.

As the month moved on, the sun's warmth was lost in the cold of the air, despite its direct brightness. The call of the rooks rode the flow and ached away. Light pierced every gap, arrowing the hedgerows as I arrived at Brook Hollows. The stillness of the lake shared the colour of the sky and the feeding brook repeated the canopy into a grand hollow of green that the sun behind could not pierce. A beat of birdcalls, pitch raised, threaded the growth as the evening tried to share my warmth. The air was the cool breath of autumn yet the martins still carried summer trails above the meadow. Returning, dozens of migrating swallows came low, like a description of a gale, over fields and hedgerows, rapid and direct. Then, from their distant perch, hidden rooks bled their calls into the air of changing season until they took to it, black against the stained horizon.

It was the middle place between summer and autumn. Stranded between seasons at Anslow Park the landscape seemed reduced; pool still, trees lacking presence. Mildew on distant young oak appeared like glints on the gloss of summer, but the closer truth was curled and spoke of endings. The birch rippled with applause as two dozen spears of purple spires blazed. A single bird repeated a single note as the exchange of season dripped by. And that note followed me, on to the higher ground where the young plantation was beginning to obscure the wider view of the Trent valley, such that little built could be seen and the road noise was the only intrusion, but the constant repeat of that one note drew my attention away until I occupied that middle space with the season. On my return, the pond seemed like two identical sides of that middle place, or the past and future, with the present being the image in my mind alone. I felt the weight and cold of the pooled water as it sank in the landscape where the eternity of being has a home.

This blackbird's year continued at Kedleston Hall, where art had been installed about the parkland. Atop a hill, a sculpted horn of mindful attention gathered the sky and I could hear a summer of insects and, of all things, simmering sausages. Close-by, thirty-one beech, reduced to a prime by those fallen, stood within twenty-five yards of a central point. A place that can be viewed from the outside, seeing one's own extended mind, or move within and be a minds eye within a mind viewing another place. How a salient clump of trees mix subject and object, bringing a different mind, a seemingly haunted self to a hilltop. With mind folding in upon itself I left and found the temporal extent of the ancient oak, which extends the mind in time, with its centuries of growth, maturity and decay.

A few days of rain later, with river contained above the plain, the oxbow was swollen, engaging with new ground, surrounding stumps to islands, touching trees through their branches. Contorted stems stood crooked, awaiting shepherds. Finches crazed the air in flight and sound, above where the meadow lay pooled. Each time a finch extended its wings they caught the low sun, eclipsing it with a blink of feathered light. A robin sang unseen to another, hidden beyond foliage massed by bees. A wren tapped out its metallic message from arching stems of willow, their olive streaked leaves in forlorn motion above, describing ellipses in the air. The painter's alder appeared to rest upon the risen water as waterfowl enjoyed new found expanse. There was a still calm over the water meadows, drawn by the extended sky and reflected in the oxbow such that I was the sensing vessel sailing the landscape of being.

I saw September out at Corbett's Wood, a plantation towards the heart of Needwood. The blue-green grass held silver strings of beaded rain as it lay, revealing the direction of the week's gales. The remaining breeze sounded the birch, that were shot with spent yellows. As the wind demanded more the pale young trunks swayed as did the splayed branches, dark, yet bright uppers from sun above. The rides allowed my progress and I looked deep into the heart of the young wood, where only the birch demanded attention, their sun mottled trunks upright through a maze of branches. Where space allowed, the sky covered all and warmth seemed to pool in the clearings, the treetops fanning the cooling breeze away. A lichen-clasped verbena burst into a rage of red flamed leaves and stood, erupting from the green. Nearby, as if caught by the heat, a group of ash stood like burnt shadows; bare apart from a few dark leaves, curled as they'd withered. I moved on, into the fields where jackdaws around a mature ash gave a sound for each falling leaf. Rooks rose and returned as leaves released. Others gathered in the field, notes on staves of cut rows playing autumn.

In Brook Hollows, reflected ash bled into the October sky, drops of foliage disappearing into the mirrored world. Silted isles gathered flotsam and where the water was most still it repeated the landscape, bringing depth where there were shallows. A robin explored the woods with sound while a blackbird lost its darkness in the holly; and each step became another line in the story of the day. The sound of movement and peace of still wrapped my progress such that I moved with the wood. And where the wind moved with the wood I found the place where it ended and became open fields. Where a galaxy of pinks perched on straggled clover about four meadow oaks. Cued by place, the patterns of the swallows left my memory and with one mind became as real as they had been, and the curiosity of their form engaged me.

Writing nature is an interaction, a sharing of place and ultimately being a voice to the landscape itself; not that the human is special and can give voice, but the human as part of nature can provide a voice.

Our self is just part of a wider being, as integrated zooids create a Man o' War. Allow the landscape to speak to you, for nature always has a story to tell. The sun can light a different chapter in one place, as can the rain, breeze and sky; time and orbit. Our steps are new lines and in one hundred paces, a hundred stories can be told. Each passing bird and leaf unfurled is a new word in nature's story. In Mind and Nature, Gregory Bateson writes of stories in all life and mind; stories as patterns through time. Stories of growth, evolution and life, and we forget that our lives, behaviour and actions are stories insignificant in the wonder of the whole. Stories that provide the context for what comes next, whether it be a tree reaching for light or a hawk chasing its prey.

When one becomes familiar with the local landscape it can also tell of stories past. The landscape becomes an external memory in a shared mind, each haunt a scene full of cues. Many cues, as leaves on a tree. Each path, plantation and tree, each flower, grass and bird, is connected to another time. Each scent and reflection, each cloud and gust of wind, both a present connection and memory weaving your self into the landscape; all through being in the landscape.

To Dunstall, in a light so sharp that it might cut the retina; images of the landscape were engraved in the mind's eye that is also the landscape itself. In the shade of the woods, the snow berries held the cool of the night and a few held rain drops that had coated the berry with a sheen that made the sphere apparent. To be in the landscape when it was at peace under keen light was a brake on progress. Each leaf, twig and droplet of dew engaged the light and a brown argus butterfly scattered about as a spent leaf given flight. The light chiselled each leaf to a gemstone; crisp, sharp and shadowed, they shimmered with content. Shadows, like hollows expertly hewn from the land, rode the contours long. A dozen finches about a rowan left against the sun, the wing filtered light engraving itself on the day, a super nova bursting from the silhouetted tree. From raised vantage, the land seeped away, as waves of subdued calm after a storm. And the ash were particularly keen to describe the beauty of the day. I felt the peaks of summer retreating to a flat calm of winter, as vigour and splendour sank and regressed to the horizon. Entering the woods was like rejoining a host, a mothership floating amongst the vacuum of farmed fields. And there at the edge of the wood, with the breeze free to travel across expanse, I felt lifted to a flight of fancy above the trees, looking down on the tree tops still bathed in the stream of evening light, meeting the skylark, mouth agape for a flow of tears that are sound. And they dropped, purple and flamed, melted and trailing a spiral strand of sooty vapours that had stained the day before. And as this vision built, the birds about me gave the wood a shape of sound that wrapped me up, until flown I returned to ground. Where, for fear of being stitched by blackbirds alarm into the tapestry of woodland, I fled to clear ground where I could feel human in the landscape, rather than nature as one.

Over at Brankley, a squirrel ran the hedgerow ash and hawthorn, channelled by the field boundaries to linear habits and progress. The days engaging brightness had been stolen by interfering cloud and the landscape was a cool impression of what it could be. I paced between the grown birch, an Other making progress, a discomfort in surrounding calm acceptance. Birch tell the story of the day so well, the first to feel breath, ready to receive autumn and a winter form that describes a landscape. In their midst, I stood and the day became real. The deeper the breath the more they can voice. And they told me that there would be a return to brightness and they would also come to hold the story of the rains, in multiple lenses that capture all that is visible. I moved on, being in the ancient wood stole my words, and I emerged to find a teasel that had held on to summers lilac and rested like a fallen star amongst the spent margins. Thorned bracts arced to protect the core of summer and its intense moment of glory. Close by, darker cousins had their cores explored by the return of brightness, as the birch had foretold.

Later, back at Brook Hollows, cluster upon cluster of changing leaves hung billowing about the solid, hidden cores that will soon bare inspection, free of hanging shroud. Water, launched from artificial human heights, accelerated leaves towards an edge clasping flow. And where the falling waters streamed they carried light and attempted its burial, only for it to rise and ferment in crazed release. The grey sky and tanned lake of recent rains gripped the island willow and it crept, herniated from the land, across the surfaced lake, riding a slick of shadow that seeped from the inner darkness of the wood, as nearby by the sunken stream carried a slick of light back to the heart of the wood. A conveyor of light, taken, to be digested and returned black.

By the lake, hidden sinew, fibered muscle and calcified rods of bone stood in the form of a swan. Hollow shafted calamus plunging the flesh where enriched liquid pumped via beating heart to give and receive. A fleshy cupped brain signalled the preen and step, the tail, voice and taking to the water; the curving of the neck. And that body dragged its mind away, leaving me a periphery as its mind-world centred in the lake where feeding came through making sense of the world, just here, at the edge of the wood. Crows in free flight were reflected as they crossed two skies and the exiting flow engaged neurones, such that my mind shared the stream flowing unseen. Taking my thinking, through making sense, to a flow of nature entering by my senses and exiting via my fingertips to the screen I write. And what of the swan, reflected there?

And then I shared the coming of light rain in the centre of the wood. A pleasure dome tapped out in form by leaves engaging with individual drops, until a while later those bonded atoms dropped to mass as one on my skin. A focus of smooth cool, that sits, another domed form, refracting the light from above the canopy, which stepped from darks to golds about black veins of branch, which fell through one another to the anchoring trunk, earth bound by unseen adventuring veins within the flesh of the Earth, as feathers in the swan now unseen, but sharing mind. On occasion, a leaf dropped to lie before me and a bird would call, but these simple actions split the still calm as rocks through glass. Disturbed, I moved on, out of the wood into a new light. That light that wraps a warm dusk hue about eastern faces and suggests finding clearings to the west to view morphed to grey clouds with their bases sketched pink.

Then came an hour of dusk. An unsteady line of horizon greyed the divide where clouds step irregular and land rolls to meet. Oaks, ash and field maple retired, free of spotlight to cut their image, lazily stirred by a reformed breeze not looking to steal their leaves, yet. Slow paced progress of the ending day instilled its want and I felt the call of wider plains, where space sits astride a cutting flow. Where limes, with hearts of gold worn high, sank silvered trunks into heavy clays with roots grasping rounded stones. Buried rocks, from place unknown idle beneath ground, unseen fists of place, punches held solid in those clays and seamed beds of rivers past. While I ached at the withdrawal of the day, the landscape and trees upon it sank calmly into fading light; eruptions of black cloud held around their standing vents, where buried Earth surfaces to explode at the interface of space and land in that precious film of life we skate, led by the film of consciousness that wraps our being and makes our actions purposeful.

The next morning, mists dissolved and a metallic light gradually sharpened the landscape; trees nearby were chiselled into form as those far ghosted into view. The river started to shine and eddies at a curve traced downstream, their convergence mapped. The enormity of the river, its relentless progress and solidity within its banks; an exposed vein of Earth that is calm within that calm of the flatlands surrounding. Open plains, hills and woods, but the river can add place to them all.

I stood within the curve of the river, where it speaks of its bed. I saw that our being creates an inside that says an outside exists. And out there seven minds of swan passed the painter's alder, linear, pausing at the edge of the reeds to feed. I reflected on the alder's mind, slowly making sense of the world, growing outwardly to light and sending roots to moisture, responding to the season. In their time, all plants are highly sensitive and dynamic; competitive and active in their search for resources. Large, older trees can support young trees through underground fungal networks, transporting nutrients and water. Our purposeful consciousness and anthropocentric nature can make us think that the only mind is human mind. Our being creates a self that says nature is an Other.

I looked out over the flat drizzle grey expanse, my peripheral vision embraced by the water behind. Hundreds of grey daubed trees cushioned the horizon as the river maintained its discourse with the willows and I realised at that moment I was this place; and lifted by the day, smiled. The thrill of being part of nature, feeling the flight of birds and the trace of falling leaves across one's mind. The birdsong weaving an extended self into the landscape. The steadfastness of the oak anchoring mind and being bound to that place.

Flat equates to still, and there, with the stillness of the weather, light and landscape, place became so peaceful it seemed to take another form. A vibrant energy that not only extended the mind, but also dragged it out with such intensity that the cluster of a dozen maple here, became a barred haven in which to secure and bound thought itself. Rescued, I fled the stillness and space through tunnels of hawthorn, only to be confronted by a pink dusk igniting the fading willow. A scalded heron leapt as a magpie fanned the flames. The day was done.

Chapter 9

Flatlands

24th October to 18th November

"The exceeding beauty of the earth, in her splendour of life, yields a new thought with every petal." – Richard Jefferies

At Brook Hollows, the wind released leaves from high on the sycamore. Some spiralled down, stalk first to puncture the water and then float, bobbing and pecking at the water like the fowl beyond. They floated with the breeze until they cupped water and slowly submerged. The willow beyond launched canoe like forms that stayed afloat, crossing the lake on the breeze to gather in the bay of the isle, as above, gulls gathered in an apery of discontent. The normally dark stream threaded through drifts of lime, becoming a flow of highlighted bronze that wrapped itself in gold.

On land, the clearings were more leaf than earth and a decoration of fallen ash challenged the gloom. A beech harboured light within its distributed branches. Its calmness of space lighting the fading leaves to a revival. The thin dark branches becoming a prominent force, as they spanned an area of woodland out of proportion to their slender girth. It is a tree that could shelter a choir, but neither they, nor a blackbird, could sing its compelling form.

I moved on and set out along a golden tubular wood to a place where moss and reddening briers cross war-time concrete, standing like veins through creeping green flesh. Joints flourished with arching grasses and occasional upright dried forms that gave witness to the breeze. A frieze of autumn lime were vibrant before water logged fields that rolled away to obscurity in the mists. Puddles in the clay brought steel flatness to furrows that led the eye away from the playful lime. Their heart forms agitated by the wind to fibrillation as they accepted the coming fall to join the sodden soils.

At Anslow Park days later, the reeds released themselves to the breeze, which was bringing the first of winter's chill. Young oak tumbled away, bursts of flak towards fired birch spattered against the horizon, an exit wound of summer. A cherry was near fully bared, a few drops of colour hung, each leaf its own rather than a foliage. Close by a robin sang, each note became a drop of colour, an autumnal leaf until it too was bare and the remaining leaves tried to respond as they moved with the rush of cold air. On the ridge the young ash were curling to black from green, a fungal exit of decay. Not accompanied by a fanfare, just the rook's description of a landscape scarred.

I visited the hollows each day in increasingly cool Autumnal conditions. Walking the paths without destination, tunnelled by the fleshy veins to the heart of the wood, and that harbouring beech was a gift to my eyes each day, its space seemed to hold me, or be my mind.

I chose to see out October in more extensive flatlands and returned to Norfolk, where landscape becomes a disc world, played by the laser light of the setting sun amidst a wind of rapid rotation and the reeds make a perennial request for silence; the quiet needed to contemplate this place. Surrounded by a flat, extended horizon, the mind streams to it, taking in a solar system where trees are planets and we are sun. But just because we occupy the centre of our mind does not mean we are the centre of this world and that it is our resource. As I stood at the centre of my disc world, the moon rose in the east like a projection of the sun and it was time to move on.

As I walked, blackbirds dived and crossed the berried channels. Hips of dog rose, red with hanging lanterns of the day's rain, attached to thorned stems that looped about blackberry briers. The reeds had their silence and the blackbirds respected it, but the robin couldn't help sing of the day and then the reeds asked for silence once more. Redshank, fashioned from silvered bark, held firm in the air, above the salt marsh that seems to soak light into its drabness, only for it to seep away in silvered channels through the mud. Other birds of the marsh passed with falcon wings, simple repeated calls as melancholy as the bleak coast. Each note a stitch uniting mind to the fabric of this place.

The next day at Cley, dozens of birds rose from saline lagoons within the reeds; as bright, dense and many as the leaves of white poplar. Lapwings, beating black and white, looped within the storm. And with time, the birds brought dimensions to the linear landscape, single points of crow and the scattered blackness of approaching flocks, morphing and splitting form. Four brent geese sprinted in.

In the stillness, watched, the reeds became the line of bare trees beyond, until the water was ringed by falling rain. The shower grew to a beating as new light lifted the grey, bringing forth autumn colours and a rainbow above bleeding white birch. And each drop of rain, at one moment in its arrival, became a point of sunlight, and all the while jays passed and the landscape was more than that it held within.

By sundown there was silent progress of orange-lit gulls, from land to coast before starlings brought the sound of the wind. Small pools became fragments of sky and the leaves of reeds became arrows of light, as walking the dusk the flatland curled in under a raw scar sunset. An egret became ghost, lost to the fading light and alarm calls of dusk rose with the smoke of settlement beyond. Life about the marsh was in sharp focus and I accepted it without troubling identification, until, a kingfisher appeared and hovered on the wind, a brilliant bead spinning above the reeds. I stayed for the arrivals as light left. Stood, an unseen flock of starlings arrived overhead, accompanied by an implosion and deep evacuation of sound. Night.

In the flatlands, day and place were still and a cold slab of sky became a shell of mind waiting to be populated. I looked out onto this new day until the greys came together to form a gull, its passing dynamic in the stillness. Its mind warped space and teased a strand of mine towards it, puncturing the still shell. The perceptual deprivation of the uniform sky altered my consciousness and I retreated to find structure in the woods.

Back home, despite the cold, the autumn foliage seemed to be melting, dripping down in two dimensions, as water on glass. On the horizon, my favourite slender tree was tissue cut, such that it might float away if there were a breeze. And onward, the trees formed like vapours in a nebula light. Exploring the landscape, I felt that I must stop at a place where the trees had an intensity of mind. The landscape whale-backed to a place where birch cried autumn, crows became singularities and ash trees stood like ghosts of their future selves.

There were waves of larch, their boughs like cloths of honour behind a hawthorn throne. The colour of the oaks added new dimensions to the compassionate forms hanging above each stout pillar of strength. The mighty beech let the sky through and the water beaded lime shone with the misted sun, as the hedgerows and grasses glittered through the matt air. An air that held its place and sat across the landscape, carrying the closing sounds and scents of autumn; it lay like the rolling woods breaking onto the fields. The sun touched this disintegrating scene with a gentle light and the air seemed to want to support, rather than tease the view apart.

Within the wood were many maple, young trees reaching towards the old, their smooth barked trunks merging away through a warmth of yellow splashed leaves to create a palpable vision that could be grabbed and consumed, such was its effortless complexity and depth. It grabbed mind, and made a place to stop and share and be fed until life made sense.

Out of the woods and into a new plantation, spires of young ash, topped by a final bouquet of leaves, stood proud amongst the dressed oak. A scattered burst canopy of white poplar arched beyond, as bright in the day as a firework in darkness. Close by, a beech burst a shrapnel of new copper-alloys around its violent flurry of branches, stained two tone from recent rains. It was a place to stand still and long, to feel the pause between breaths and beats of the season. An old oak stood too, a reminder of nature's time. Here, within the landscape and slowed to nature's pace, the local chimes of noon came and seemed rapid as alarm.

The short days kept me close to home and autumn was a season turning to decay until I passed a row of young maple, standing above a floor of yellow, so intense that it seemed to make the grey sky blue. A winter wind was still laying the covering down and tree bound leaves were agitated by the luminance. The grassed lane through the fields was a fury of coloured pellets puncturing the soaked drabness. The boughs of gold were explored by the darkness of a snag oak, its damp stained branches twisting about the flakes of colour, bare and avoiding.

I visited a pool close by that rarely requests my presence. It sat cornered, balancing the field, balanced by the oak on its bank and by those oak marking the hedgerows beyond. In turn, the water balanced the sky and the leaves balanced in the reflective surface. And within this equilibrium I knew exactly where I should stand. And there I stood within this landscape whole. When I left, it was the right time to leave and from all other elsewheres the aesthetic and mind of that place was lost.

Gregory Bateson saw the link between aesthetic and mind, the products of nature having a natural beauty that is a mind within our mind, we perceive a relationship to it such that it is an extension of our own sense of self. There are places within the patterns of landscape and mind with aesthetic appeal, and these places are often worn to by pathways of foot until, in some cases, they are encased, like exhibits, surrounded by concrete laid down to cover our pathways of human habit; habit to view and be within the aesthetic.

I carried on and arrived at a place where the noise of speeding asphalt masked the countryside. It beat my senses for sometime, until a pathway through the fields to rookery wood became clear. Here, the bare sodden earth was a place where colours died, it shone with silted pools reflecting grey skies. Nuggets of planet lay scattered in the soil, holding their form as the rooks above varied theirs in flight; pebbles of sound falling to embed in mind. I walked on and reached the woods of Brook Hollows, where each leaf fell in its own way, describing its own path. Within the wood I felt I was an organ within its being, only separated by our time scales, our branches of life and taxonomy: our self. The rain came to emphasise our shared needs and I moved on within my host.

It was mid-November and frost metalled and galvanised the ground, noting the form and structure of the lying leaves. Bare birch became beams of light, speared by the dark arrows of their branches. Fountains of summer reduced to a splash of yellow as they dived into winter. Finest twigs, filaments of charge exploring the plasma of the frost charged day. Fieldfares massed from field to tree, from tree to shrub; parts in a pattern of seen mind, never wanting to share mine, always moving on. Until they rose as one, finches, fieldfares and all to occupy the sky that spoke of winter and enclosed the setting sun behind sheet ice. Where there is nature, there is mind and as the air cooled, mists formed to enclose the senses, enclose the mind and reveal a lesser self, denied landscape.

Chapter 10

Patterns of Nature

21ˢᵗ November to New Year

"For this beautiful and wonderful light excited a sense of some likewise beautiful and wonderful truth, some unknown but grand thought hovering as a swallow above." – Richard Jefferies

A blackbird lost of voice perched where it had once found song, receiving the rain with a steady contentment, as if each drop were a note for the coming year. The newly bare oak had their revised summer forms revealed by the closing light of day, inspected intensely by the contrast, stood in quiet waiting for spring to bring mind. Four rooks flew west, their blackness morphing and shifting shape towards the static oak and vibrant edge of night where they can be lost.

With canopy bare, daylight filled the hollows and the harbouring beech had lost its possession of light. Instead, it filled space and explored the air with an array of spreading branches. The leaves that had fed on summer lay waiting to feed the earth so that they might remerge in one form or another. I left the woods and crossed the fields. With each step the earth told of its sodden state and the low midday sun floated shadows long. By rookery wood, the sky did not dance, there was no mind of swallows, just an unconscious space within a network of nature; stitched from network within network.

The wood itself was busy, long tailed tits decorated an ash and floated to my feet to rest with rapid attention. There were many, and amongst them my mind felt more theirs than my own and was compelled to stay. I stood by the brook, by a sycamore with buds already green. In trios and more, the long tailed tits spiralled branches and moved from tree to tree, until I saw maples rising like solid shafts of light, projecting shadows from within to dance on their bark.

A great spotted woodpecker, crowned, bridled face, bleeding colour from its legs and as patterned as the birdsong, surveyed the wood. A treecreeper crawled the aged birch, like bark upon bark, as it ascended the trunk, illuminating the crevices with the brightness if its breast. Its body and skull reducing to its beak, action balanced by a firm tail.

The combined song of a robin and a wren filled the air and seemed to come together to describe the systems of the dell, the elongated existence of trees, the greenery about their base, the finches, tits that scatter, the strike of a goldcrest and the squirrel flowing through. Then, from within a nearby copse, I heard what I thought was a stream, waters flowing off the sodden fields, but it was a river of birdsong from a mass of unseen fieldfares; their individual calls like streamlets over pebbles. And the sound rose and fell away.

A day of misted mind when crows are faded black. Defeated grasses escaped the oxbow beneath the sound of the unseen. Pathways of habit faded to where green became grey, and the oak were watermarks in the sky.

Heavy and sustained rains had forced waters to explore new ground. Combed grasses revealed the overnight excursions and there were streams bringing their sounds to new corners of the hollows. Logs had been carried, silted isles cleared, and the new day's sun touched every bubble floating in the remaining torrents. By the edge of the wood, looking in with the sun, I raised my gaze to the taller trees to spend some time reading their story through this small window in the wood. Crazed trunks, green against the blue, wrapped by shadow and a rotting branch that made me feel sorrow. As I contemplated its fate a peregrine arrived from the east and floated to a brief pause on the wind, its bright underside distinct. It left north, until a little while later it shot past from the west.

December, a still, resting landscape, familiar forms, but a new location in the fields of Needwood. Meadow trees stood at the centre of their fall and the blue sky became steel as the hard edge of winter promised to cut across the landscape and make nature struggle. The sodden earth was frozen, but streams still flowed; life leaching from the land, the sap of dormant trees. Ash, hawthorn and dog rose leaders fired from laid hedgerows and some waved a final hand of leaves.

A life of tired summer's growth mixed on the woodland floor beneath a discourse of hidden birds. And away from the pathways, the mounds of briers shone and I stood amidst their breaking waves. I saw a ferment of sea on a rocky shore, frozen and peaceful in time, until the sun broke through to redescribe them and bring a new vigour to the stillness. And the birds began to sing, and the trees rose high into the blue describing the fanfare below in spreading form. And there, tied in the briers, a few pink flowers of a wild geranium, their salience amplified by mind as a robin arrived to perch on a young sweet chestnut, as if to balance the place and scene.

Outside the wood, where the landscape rolled to a modest valley, a stream flowed through under blue, pulling with it strands of life as it curved in two dimensions, like the landscape in three above. A channel of mind, a whirlpool integrating self and place. Unity.

I walked from the risings until I reached a new dimensioned place. Where flood plains offer so much depth, let sun spill out and winds sheer. Where trees stand bold and intricate. Where shadow longs for river far. Where light projects self. Flooded fields lay before and beyond, the oxbow trees providing backdrop and reflection, floating the oxbow into sky. In the stillness of a flood-silted stream there was a wisp of ice, patterned like the trunk of a cherry tree, pointing up stream to where a bank of gravel had changed the flow. As I left, the arriving dusk reduced a robin to a two dimensional form, only for its song to reform its depth and identity

A mind in nature day, when the landscape seemed to know. Winter revealed how the laid hedgerows return to vertical. The hawthorn knowing, responding, making sense of the world and finding the sky. Young ash were locked in a frozen pool as others refracted the sun with liquid beads hung from the nadir of each twig; or in those places a protrusion of form affords. Just like those places where people gather, where the aesthetic form of the landscape suggests a place to stand. And beyond, that place was found.

The snowberries massed bright in their network of wiry growth, as stars in an invisibility of matter, such is their contrast. They sat in ones, or binary pairs, letting our sun describe their spheres, such that each had day and night, and each had dusk and dawn. And at their poles, they attached to their wired host or became a point of matter. Stood amongst them, they became stars in a galaxy of mind, where there is no space or time, but yet it is seen, as a mass of neurones demand it. And when that moment of peace was quietly shattered by voice, those neurones were fired by the difference and forced me to move on.

A week after my first visit I returned to the fields of Needwood. A blackbird, wings lit to silver blades, cut through the still air with alarm towards the tired hedgerow mounded with bramble. A copse of a dozen oaks, topped a hill and received the light to make shadow. The winter gloss of holly revealed its form of Bézier surfaces, like the rolling landscape beyond, patterned by shades of fallow earth enclosed. The light reached in to the heart of the wood and lit its arteries sharp and lines of brightness rose against the sky. As the path turned, its wet leaves shone and the brightness challenged my vision, trees ahead became stark coded lines and those behind became the green of the fields. A week on and the petals of the geranium flowers had curled back in the face of the frosts and were dwarfs of their former star. The young sweet chestnut where the robin perched was circled by the difference in light and threads of gossamer trailed between its twiggy growth. From the uppermost there was one dried leaf, like a scarf wired in the wind. Out of the wood, in the open of the field, I stood with a stream crossing my senses and looked out at a lone oak beyond, and that vision and sound combined to root me to a new place. Unity once more.

A grasping hand of distant summer reached across the sky with a colour that made the air itself seem flesh, and their within that all encompassing hue, the patterns that connect life and mind, cells and thought, cosmos and being were clear. And the divisions laid down by human doings became dressed, as wounds that will in time heal, but only after we are gone. The deep knowing of cosmos seemed at peace with our irritation; for we are not even grit within an eye, just dust on a sentence, in a story that will never be read.

Sky, light and cloud created a distant sea, exploring the shore before a shining horizon. A bank of cloud sailed slowly above with a keel of vectored light ploughing the depths. And I wanted to be lone in the landscape as a vessel at sea. I found that solitude in the lee of a wood, and standing there a breeze of fieldfares approached and lifted to the canopy to vanish as spray from a wave. And this place was so easy to find as so few people explore the local landscape and leave the known. And the joy of just being in the landscape, fed by the forest, consumed me as I stood.

In fading light, as the wind pulled the tired grasses that once bent to purple, a buzzard called and the contours of the gathered clouds were washed with winter's faded orange. There was little to hold onto but one's mindscape, and as when looking at the Earth from upon it, we can never know that mindscapes true form, if form is what it has. And as I passed a ribbon of trees, the trunks cut the light with each step, again and again, but how ever many times we cut and inspect the parts we will never know the story of the whole, it is sometimes best just to know that we are tied within the relationships and processes of nature, and let it be.

The sun was a viewable brightness beyond the contrast of sky and trees. Frosted pinstripe twigs caught the frozen light and explored the white air. Mind and time were still in the paused woods. By the brook, unfrozen, time flowed and life erupted in the form of birdsong that always fills this place in rookery wood.

The lightest of rain circled as I reached the oxbow and sunlight brought clarity to the fields, lighting fieldfares to the silver of reflecting water as they rippled along the hedgerows. The River Dove was busy and vocal, testing the banked trees;

the low sun highlighted where the river spoke and shaded the contours of the land. It was a place to stand, and there I saw the trees and birds as systems of matter, ever changing but always the same, like the river. Matter formed around strands of life, instructions of form, energy harnessed to create order and maintain complex structure within a universe of inevitable decay. Even in the seeming perfection of life, there is always potential for change and disorder. Until, energy lost, we disintegrate: mind ends.

As December progressed, the spines of the Earth stood stark at Anslow Park. Spears of birch rooted, their white trunks dark in reflection from the silted pond. The ground was more than sodden, each step was immersion and cleansing of feet, a ceremony of readoption by nature. As ever, the lenses of water hanging about the trees drew my attention, small domes like minds, seemingly containing their landscape, an unconscious of fluid that can never be apart from that which surrounds. The sodden land lay below still trees, the grey skies cleared to reveal a misted half moon, and a single great tit spoke of the balance of the day, a pit of solstice or the base of life. The young ash antlered the sky, and the mist before the moon fell, coating the fields, underlining the hedgerows, gathering in the shallow pockets of the land, yet still floating in reverence at the interface of states of matter. From within the pockets of mist only the boldest trees stood true.

The following day, the landscape sank under constant rains, the robin's song flowed as tears on a mountainside, round trees, and with the brook, they bled the landscapes pain for dry that went unnoticed. Torrents of winter's beige hue churned through, leaving banks and spreading flat, stranding blackened trees and making patterns of the sky. The hollows air, its earth, its trees seemed liquid and the water drowned the robin's song and drops tapped from tree to ground. The harbouring beech was a blackened green that slimed the trunk as branches balanced light on their uppers. As I walked to higher ground from the valley floor, the robin's song contained hope, coiling the mist into unseen patterns, like those that host our matter; the patterns that are tree and crab, and butterfly and man. Like a shadow cast on mist, I could almost grasp a sense of truth, but felt a perennial unknowing of those patterns that connect all and guide the trees of life, but are as visible as mind.

At Brankley, I sat in a bowl of bird sound, filled with chatter and rimmed by the song of two or three robins. A snag oak stood near, its filaments exploring the mist, a lower branch like the head of a stag exploding from its trunk, head down ready to charge down the slope. Lone crows were all that crossed the stillness, curling from trees or direct across the valley floor to be lost against the backdrop of distant, dark hedgerows where rooks dug life out of the day with their mechanical utterances of companionship. It is at these times, in this stillness and dearth of vibrancy that the landscape and nature upon it seem soaked with solace, the flight of blackness and voices of rooks asking questions we would rather not hear about decay.

It was the winter solstice and at rookery wood, in the margin of the field a dead rook lay. Blackness stripped to its white cage; but somehow conscious of its death. Its matter, coalesced and patterned about the system that was rook, released by its passing to be shared, seeping into the earth to emerge attached to life once more. Like our consciousness is the surface of a sea of mind, the rook's blackness is the conscious surface of red flesh and white bones, describing the being to our eyes, rippling our thoughts and plunging the depths of our unconscious being.

Finches peeled from the doormat hedgerows and curved with the wind to a lone oak by a small stream. Floodwaters had thatched reeds into breaking waves, but they did not speak and I felt I was mining words from the landscape, dragging them from thought rather than arriving from the process of being in nature. And within these quiet fields, inside a mindscape, I felt an end to my journey; a unity, a connection sated, an understanding of being in the landscape. And later, the mild air brought wonder to the pit of the longest night; a blackbird returned to song, its energy of tone defeating the buffeting breeze to enliven every space and surface. Each phrase a pattern where thoughts might coalesce and in some mind make an angel; a blackbird bringing news of a new year.

Acknowledgements

Special thanks to my family, for giving me the time and support needed to complete this work. To Peter Reason for the welcome and excellent guidance on the initial chapters. To friends and family for their feedback on drafts. Finally, the custodians of the landscape and natural world around Needwood and beyond: Derbyshire Wildlife Trust, Staffordshire Wildlife Trust, The National Forest, Natural England, Woodland Trust, National Trust, Blithfield Estate, Rangemore Estate, Dunstall Estate, the Duchy of Lancaster's Needwood Estate and those others who maintain the various rivers of human habit across the landscape.

Lightning Source UK Ltd.
Milton Keynes UK
UKOW03f0051211014

240407UK00004B/260/P